TAXATION FOR
AUSTRALIAN
BUSINESSES

TAXATION FOR AUSTRALIAN BUSINESSES

Understanding Australian Business Taxation Concessions

ROD CALDWELL

Wrightbooks
A Wiley Brand

First published in 2014 by Wrightbooks
An imprint of John Wiley & Sons Australia, Ltd
42 McDougall St, Milton Qld 4064

Office also in Melbourne

Typeset in 11.3/14 pt ITC Berkeley Oldstyle Std

© TPA Business Solutions 2014

The moral rights of the author have been asserted

National Library of Australia Cataloguing-in-Publication data:

Author:	Caldwell, Rod, author.
Title:	Taxation for Australian businesses: understanding Australian business taxation concessions / Rod Caldwell.
ISBN:	9780730309321 (pbk)
	9780730309352 (ebook)
Notes:	Includes index.
Subjects:	Business enterprises — Taxation — Australia.
	Small business — Taxation — Australia.
	Taxation — Australia.
Dewey Number:	336.2070994

Cover design by Wiley

Tables 5.1, 9.1, AA1, AB1, AB2 and figures 11.1, 11.4, 11.5, 11.7 © Australian Taxation Office for the Commonwealth of Australia. The ATO material included in this publication was current at the time of publishing. Readers should refer to the ATO website www.ato.gov.au for up-to-date ATO information.

Printed in Singapore by C.O.S. Printers Pte Ltd

10 9 8 7 6 5 4 3 2 1

Disclaimer

The material in this publication is of the nature of general comment only, and does not represent professional advice. It is not intended to provide specific guidance for particular circumstances and it should not be relied on as the basis for any decision to take action or not take action on any matter which it covers. Readers should obtain professional advice where appropriate, before making any such decision. To the maximum extent permitted by law, the author and publisher disclaim all responsibility and liability to any person, arising directly or indirectly from any person taking or not taking action based on the information in this publication.

For Robyn

Dedicated to my wife Robyn, without whose encouragement and support this book would not have been possible.

Contents

About the author

Rod Caldwell is a tax accountant with postgraduate qualifications in taxation. He spent 20 years with the Australian Taxation Office, where he was a tax advisor in a centre of excellence, recognised by CPA Australia as a tax specialist and awarded Fellow status. He left the Tax Office in 2005 to try his hand at teaching. Rod has lectured and tutored in taxation and management accounting at a number of Australian universities, including Monash University, University of Western Australia and Edith Cowan University, as well as teaching business studies at diploma and advanced diploma levels at a number of TAFE colleges in Western Australia. His first book was published by Wrightbooks in 2004. He currently has four books in print and another due to be released later in 2014.

Preface

While I was reading the local newspaper the other day two articles caught my attention. In one an ex-Glory football player and accountant had misappropriated money from his business in order to fund a gambling debt, and as a consequence of this he had not paid the correct amount of tax on his earnings. He was subsequently sentenced to seven years imprisonment for tax fraud, a victimless crime. In another article, a clandestine drug lab exploded, injuring the offender and a child living at the same residence. He received only five years for his efforts.

The moral to this story is that our society views crimes against the state as far more serious than crimes against the individual, even an innocent toddler. So beware the Tax Man!

In this text I will introduce you to taxation as it affects small to medium-sized businesses. Generally we are talking about businesses with a turnover under $25 million, which covers about 70 per cent of all businesses in Australia. We will also discuss the small business concessions that can be accessed by micro businesses — that is, businesses with a turnover under $2 million; the capital gains tax concessions that apply to micro and small businesses with less than $6 million in net assets; and the fringe benefits tax parking exemption that applies to business with an income of less than $10 million. Businesses with turnovers in excess of $10 million, usually referred to as Small to Medium enterprises, cannot access any taxation concessions, while those with turnovers in excess of $25 million, generally referred to as large businesses, are outside the scope of this text.

This book is not intended to supplant your tax accountant. Unfortunately our tax laws are so complex—some would say stupidly so—that the services of a tax accountant are almost mandatory for all small businesses in Australia. What I will do is empower you so you will be able to keep your records in a tax-compliant fashion, minimising the work your accountant has to do on your behalf. Accountants charge in six-minute billing units and the fewer your job requires, the less you have to pay.

One of the problems facing tax authors is that the tax rates quoted in any printed text are usually out of date by the time the book hits the shelves. The reason for this is political: our politicians cannot seem to stop themselves constantly fiddling with the tax regime to suit their own political agenda.

As an example, the small business asset write-off limit (which we discuss in chapter 4, on capital allowances) was $1000 up to the 2013 tax year, $6500 for the 2013 tax year and up to 31 December 2013, and was proposed (but is so far not legislated) to return to $1000 from 1 January 2014. This sort of tinkering makes keeping a book like this completely up to date an impossible task.

For this reason, although I have included the tax rates that were current at the time of writing, I will also publish the latest tax rates under the 'Update' link on the website for this book at www.tpabusiness.com.au, where I also maintain an errata page that will explain how the changes affect particular sections of the book itself. In this way your information will always be up to date, irrespective of when the book was published.

Additional resources for this and my other texts, including an introductory video for each chapter in this book, are available on my website. I am also happy to answer any questions you may have in relation to any of my texts at rod@tpabusiness.com.au.

Rod Caldwell
August 2014

CHAPTER 1
A general discussion of taxation

Key areas we will cover in this chapter

▶ Introduction—what this book covers

▶ Am I in business?

▶ Small business concessions

▶ The Big 4—income tax, CGT, FBT and GST

▶ State-based taxation

▶ Private use of business assets

▶ Bookkeeping and recording systems

Defined terms we will introduce

Micro business: used to mean a small business with a turnover under $2 million

Small business: used in this text to mean a business with a turnover in excess of $2 million but under $25 million

Small to medium business (SME): used to mean a business with a turnover in excess of $10 million but under $25 million

Large proprietary (private) company (as defined by ASIC): a Pty Ltd company that satisfies any two of the following: revenue > $25m; assets > $12m; and employs over 50 staff

Small business concessions: a set of tax concessions available to micro businesses with a turnover under $2 million

'Turnover': the aggregate total of all income made by the business from the provisions of goods or services, including your total sales, fees and commissions

Simplified tax system: now replaced by the small business tax concessions

Income tax: a tax on net income, on a sliding scale for individuals (progressive), fixed for companies (flat)

CGT (capital gains tax): a tax on profits made from the disposal of an asset

FBT (fringe benefits tax): a tax on benefits provided to business owners and employees

GST (goods and services tax): a flat tax on the provision of most goods and services (basic foodstuff and financial services are among the exemptions)

BAS (Business Activity Statement): a form part filled, sent to businesses by the Tax Office, usually quarterly, used as a method of payment for a number of taxes: Income Tax, FBT, withholding and the GST.

IAS (Income Activity Statement): a form part filled by the Tax Office, sent to businesses not registered for the GST. It serves the same purpose as the BAS but without the GST component

Payroll tax: a state-based tax on your total payroll. There is a minimum threshold (different for each state) under which no tax is payable.

Duties: the new term for state-based stamp duties, usually levied on the purchase of property, motor vehicles and insurance, which differ between states

Is it really worth staying in business? Australian businesses feel so overwhelmed by paperwork that many consider giving up, while the 'experts' say that the trick to getting on top of your tax obligations is to become educated and informed. The objective of this book is to give you the knowledge and the tools that will allow you to maintain your day-to-day accounting records in such a way that your tax requirements are met with as little additional work as possible.

In the book I will discuss the process of keeping your accounting records in order so that you will comply with the taxation provisions, rather than comply with general accounting concepts, today known as the International Financial Reporting Standards or IFRS. What is the difference? Historically the tax acts have been written with little or no regard to generally accepted accounting principles! Fortunately these principles are of little use to small businesses, provided that the method used by the business to account for its business activities gives a true and fair view of the entity's financial position.

To make the book easier to read, I will as far as possible use plain English, as distinct from the jargon often favoured by accountants. For example, I use *depreciation* rather than the more technically correct term *decline in value*. I do not say 'you may deduct an amount to the extent that is used to produce your assessable income' but rather use the term *business expense*.

Is this book for you?

The text assumes that you are a small to medium-sized business with a turnover of up to $25 million, operating as an individual or partnership, as a private company (Pty Ltd) or as a trustee of a family trust. These different tax structures are discussed in depth in later chapters.

Further, I will also assume that you may be eligible to use the taxation concessions for small business (previously called the *simplified tax system*); that is, you deal with the Australian Taxation Office (Tax Office) on a cash basis for both income tax and the GST. However, as you will read a little later on, the bar to entry to these concessions is set fairly low, therefore I will also be discussing the tax positions of small businesses that are ineligible to access these concessions. Small businesses that can take advantage of these concessions because they have an annual turnover under $2 million I will refer to as *micro businesses*, and those with a turnover above $2 million that cannot access these concessions I will refer to as *small businesses*.

I should highlight a point of confusion here. There is no fixed definition of a small business; rather, wherever this term is used it is defined for that purpose. Small businesses with a turnover under $2 million are often called micro businesses; those with a turnover between $2 million and $10 million and with net assets under $6 million are defined as small; those between $10 million and $25 million are defined as small to medium (SME); while those with a turnover of over $25 million that satisfy the 'large proprietary' definition are referred to as large. It has also been proposed that large private companies will have additional reporting requirements placed on them by ASIC that will take them outside the scope of this text.

There are many concessions available to micro businesses. My principal objective is to help you to keep you records in such a manner that you take full advantage of these concessions and, further, that your accountant does not need to spend time reworking them to meet the taxation requirements. This will help to reduce your accounting fees while increasing your knowledge and understanding of the tax accounting requirements of your business.

Conservative advice

The advice given in this book tends to be on the conservative side. By this I mean that some tax accountants can be more aggressive in their approach to accounting for tax purposes. If you use this book as a 'bookkeeping guide', then you will be on a very solid footing for tax, including GST, FBT and income tax. It is not intended to completely replace the professional advice of your accountant or financial advisor. Rather, it serves as a guide that will empower you when it comes time to deal with these professionals or, if you wish, empower you to DIY.

One fact that is not generally understood by the small business community, however, is that in dealing with the Tax Office, a tax agent acts on your behalf. It is as though his actions are your actions. If the agent makes excessive claims to reduce your tax bill, those claims are your claims. The Tax Office will come to your door for an explanation and give you the bill (possibly with interest and up to 200 per cent penalties). You will not be able to hide behind your tax agent and will be held 100 per cent responsible.

The moral of this is that it is better to be a little conservative and be able to sleep at night rather than make suspect claims and be forever waiting for the knock at the door!

Am I in business?

What a silly question, of course I'm in business...well, maybe not?

A business, sometimes called an enterprise for tax purposes, is usually thought of as any money-making activity you undertake. However, the

Tax Office has a number of rules to determine if you are 'in business' for tax purposes. The purpose of the restrictions, as far as the Tax Office is concerned, is twofold. They are intended, firstly, to prevent you from claiming business losses against other income and, secondly, to prevent normal salary and wages being 'alienated'—that is, passed through a business structure to other family members in order to reduce your tax burden.

The general rule is: if you intend to make a profit, other than profit incidental to a hobby activity, then you are in business. The courts have tried to come to terms with this concept but have failed to establish any absolute rules. Owning one goat may be a business activity while owning six cattle may not. It all depends on your real intention when you set out on this activity. Its scale, planning, business structure and profit-making purpose are all factors that will contribute to determining whether or not you are 'in business' for taxation purposes.

If you run at a loss, but have a reasonable expectation of profit, you may be in business, but if there is no reasonable expectation of profit, the Tax Office would not consider you to be in business. In these cases, you may need to seek a professional opinion as to whether or not you can claim your losses against your other income, such as against your salary or wages from other activities.

Another test is that you must be involved in an 'active' business. Owning a rental property is not normally considered to be a business activity, neither is owning a share portfolio or other 'passive' investments. However, you can usually deduct your excess expenses associated with these activities from other income, normally wages or salaries. This is referred to as *negative gearing*.

This book, however, is aimed at 'true' business activities that are actively undertaken by the owners, such as managing a small deli, operating as a home-based contractor or running a small shop, rather than at loss-making hobbies or passive investments.

Whether or not you are in business, you will need to keep accurate business records. 'Hobby' businesses tend to develop into full-grown businesses. Passive investments, such as investment properties that allow negative gearing, require full business records. Apart from those activities that could be considered a true hobby, and especially if you run at a profit, the best course of action is to assume that you are in business until you are challenged. In this way you will not fall foul of withholding tax issues. As always, the first rule is if you are in any doubt, seek professional assistance.

Rental properties

A person who simply co-owns an investment property or several investment properties is usually regarded as an investor who is not carrying on a rental property business, either alone or with the other co-owners. This is because of the limited scope of the rental property activities and the limited degree to which a co-owner actively participates in rental property activities.

Non-commercial losses

So you pass all of these 'tests' but, like most small businesses, in the first few years you tend to run at a loss. Are these losses deductible against your other income, such as your salary from your day job? Unfortunately the quick answer is no!

There is another test that relates to small, loss-making ventures. If you are an individual, or in partnership, and your gross income for the year is less than $40 000, any loss you make on that activity will *probably* have to be carried forward until you make a profit. That is, you cannot deduct your losses from the business activity against other income such as your wages. When you eventually make a profit you can then deduct your carry forward losses from that profit. Exemptions to the requirement include a business that has more than $500 000 in real property under management or $100 000 worth of assets (excluding motor vehicles), or that has made a profit in three of the last five years (that profits test again!).

You must 'defer' the losses, and you are allowed to claim them only from future profits made from that enterprise. The good news is that if your income is from passive investment, such as a rental property or shares, then this test does not apply to you and you can, under normal circumstances, deduct your losses from other income—so-called negative gearing.

Am I a contractor? Am I in the business of contracting?

If I am employed then I am an 'employee' and am not 'in business'. But what if I leave my employer on Friday and am rehired as a contractor on Monday—am I now in the business of contracting?

The basic answer to this proposition is that from the viewpoint of the Tax Office, you are still an employee and are not in business. You are receiving personal services income and will declare it as such in your individual tax return. This book does not apply to contractors in this situation.

If you are looking at this question from *the employer's perspective*, then even though your 'contractor' provides you with an ABN tax invoice, you may still have to provide that employee with superannuation guarantee payment, if they are still an employee for superannuation purposes, even though they are not an employee for income tax withholding purposes.

But what if you are a 'brickie' who supplies your own equipment and contracts out to a number of builders, or a franchise courier who works for only the one company but supplies your own vehicle and so on? These classes of contractor are in business and this book applies to you. So what's the difference? Where does the Tax Office draw the line?

This book applies to you if your income is not received as a reward for personal effort or skills—that is, you're not in an employee-type situation—or if the majority (more than 75 per cent) of your income falls into one of the following categories:

▶ You obtain your income from the production of a result, for example delivering a software package rather than programming services.

▶ You are required to provide your own equipment and tools of trade, as in the case of a bricklaying contractor.

▶ You are responsible for any defects in the result. You warrant the job and must fix any problems at your own expense.

Or if no more than 80 per cent of your income comes from one client and:

▶ you have two or more clients who are unrelated to each other, and you advertise your services to the public at large, or

▶ you employ persons to do at least 20 per cent of your principal work (this does not include such tasks as your bookkeeping but is work related to your main income source), or

▶ you work from your own business premises rather than those of your employer.

Provided that you pass one of the above tests, you are 'in business'. If you are unsure, *seek professional assistance* to determine your exact position.

TFN, ABN, GST, PAYG withholding

Australian tax language is full of acronyms, many of which you will come across on a daily basis. Wherever I use these I will first define their meaning. We will start with the most common of all, the TFN.

TFN (tax file number)

If you are an individual in business you use your own tax file number for dealing with the Tax Office. If you operate through a partnership or company, however, then you will need a separate tax file number (TFN) for your business. Companies (MyCompany Pty Ltd) are first registered with (created by) the Australian Securities and Investments Commission (ASIC) and are given an Australian Company Number (ACN).

ABN (Australian business number)

Every business must register for an ABN. Without this you cannot give a tax invoice and any business purchaser of your goods or services will be required to withhold 49 per cent of the invoice amount. This will not affect a hobby business selling to the public through a market stall, say, but it will affect a business such as a school cleaning service.

Registering for the goods and services tax (GST)

If you have, or expect to have, an annual turnover in excess of $75 000 you must register for the GST. However, if you are under this amount you may still find it useful to register. There are a number of reasons for this, some of which are tax related (for example, you export goods) and some are for appearance's sake—that is, if you are not registered then you reveal yourself to be a small player and less 'worthy'. Also, some companies will not deal with an entity that is not registered for GST as they cannot claim back the GST credits for goods or services purchased from an unregistered entity.

All businesses, whether registered for the GST or not, are required to fill in a quarterly BAS unless specifically exempted, but there are ways of simplifying this task. The GST will be discussed in detail in chapter 9.

PAYG withholding

Withholding taxes are those amounts payable by others that you withhold from their payment. The most common form of withholding is the income tax deductions that you withhold from your staff wages. If you are going to employ any staff or pay wages, you must also register for PAYG withholding. You can do this at the same time as you get your ABN number.

How do I register?

The business entry point website at www.business.gov.au has a link to registration for small businesses that will lead you through the process.

► If your business is a partnership or company you will need a TFN.

► You will also need an ABN for the business.

► If you qualify for the GST, or wish to do so, you will need to register for the GST.

► If you wish to employ staff you will need to register for withholding tax.

The 'Big 4'

This book focuses primarily on four taxes:

► income tax

► capital gains tax (CGT)

► fringe benefits tax (FBT)

► goods and services tax (GST).

Unlike in other countries, in Australia the capital gains tax is covered by the *Income Tax Assessment Act* but the *Fringe Benefits Tax Assessment Act* is a separate although closely aligned piece of legislation. The *GST Act* stands completely alone, independent of the other taxing statutes. This fragmented system can lead to problems.

As an example, cash accounting under the GST applies to all sales and purchases, including sales and purchases of your business assets, whereas cash accounting under income tax applies only to income and expenses and not to assets. For example, if you purchase a computer system you can claim the GST the moment you pay for it; however, you can claim 'depreciation' of the asset only once it is installed and ready for use. This is despite the fact that you are using 'cash' as your method of accounting for both the GST and income tax. See page 50 for further information on cash accounting.

Wherever such inconsistencies in approach arise, we will attempt to advise you of the problem and lead you through the accounting maze that results.

Income tax

You pay income tax on your net business 'profit'—your taxable income—on an annual basis. The term *net* means there are some income and expense items that are neither included in your taxable income nor allowed as a taxation deduction. The best example of this is the private use deductions that will be discussed in chapter 7.

The percentage of tax you pay as an individual is based on a sliding scale that increases with your taxable income. This is referred to as a progressive taxation system, as distinct from a flat rate system. It is designed to give tax relief to low income earners, but as a result loads the burden of tax onto the higher income individuals. Companies, on the other hand, pay a flat rate of tax from their first dollar earned.

How you pay depends on your business structure:

▶ Individuals in business as sole traders include their business details in their own personal tax return (business items section). *You then pay income tax at individual rates based on your total income.*

▶ A partnership will submit an annual partnership tax return that explains to the Tax Office how the business's taxable income is to be split between the partners, although you do not pay any tax on the partnership income at this time. Each individual partner then includes their proportion of the business income in their personal tax return. *You then pay income tax at individual rates based on your total income.*

▶ A company will pay a flat rate of 28.5 per cent on their taxable income when they lodge their company tax return. You pass this income and tax on to yourself as a shareholder along with the 'franked dividend' (see chapter 10) and include the gross (pre-tax) dividend in your personal tax return along with the tax 'credit'. *You then pay income tax at individual rates based on your total income less any deductions.* This is a uniquely Australian system.

A little maths will tell you that, on the whole, whichever structure you use, your final income tax bill will be the same.

Some special income tax rules apply to some industries. For example, those engaged in primary production get special consideration, artists have special income averaging rules and prospectors have very generous capital allowance rules.

Income tax is paid at the individual level for sole traders and partnerships and at the business level for companies. It is paid as an estimate on your IAS/BAS each quarter and is not a deductible expense to your business. Each year you must complete an annual income tax return on which you will receive a credit for the tax paid, and this will form the basis of the tax estimate for the next 12 months.

Fringe benefits tax (FBT)

Fringe benefits tax is payable only where an employee receives personal enjoyment from company assets or obtains a personal benefit from company funds. Owners of companies also fall into the category of 'employees'. Individuals in business and partners are not 'employed' by their businesses and therefore have no FBT liabilities.

As fringe benefits is a tax on employee benefits it is discussed in full in chapter 7, which examines the concept of 'personal use' as well as salaries and wages.

You report your fringe benefits amounts to the Tax Office in an annual return due in March each year. The Tax Office will then include one-quarter of this amount on your BAS for the following year. The next year's FBT return will be the amount you owe less the estimates paid on your quarterly BAS.

As FBT is a tax on salary perks, it is deductible to the business and should be included with the other salary expenses. If any employee receives more than $1000 per year in FBT it must be shown on their annual payment summary.

Goods and services tax (GST)

The GST applies only to taxpayers who have registered for it. You must register if your business income exceeds $75 000, although you may register if it is under this amount and you need to issue tax-inclusive invoices to your clients. Only tax-inclusive invoices can be used to claim a tax credit.

The GST is payable on the difference between the GST you collect and the GST you pay. All income and all expenses of the business are included, with two exceptions:

▶ If your invoice does not include an amount of GST (because the supplier is not registered or the goods are not taxable), then you cannot claim a tax credit on the purchase.

▶ If there is a private use component in the payment, you can only claim the GST credit on the business use. The same applies to income items such as a trade-in or the sale of a business asset used partly for private purposes.

Basically the GST applies to *every* transaction that your business undertakes, both buying and selling, expense and income. Among the very few exceptions are basic foodstuffs, exported goods that are exempt and financial transactions by the bank, such as interest and some government charges.

Some special GST rules apply to some businesses. For example, taxi owners must register for the GST irrespective of turnover, deli owners have a special method of calculating their GST liability, and special rules also apply to vendors of second-hand goods.

Chapter 9 discusses this complex topic more fully.

Withholding taxes

These are the tax amounts owed by others to the Tax Office that you withhold from their payments. The most obvious is the income tax payable by your employees that you withhold from their salary. In the case of suppliers who cannot provide you with a tax invoice stating their ABN number, the amount of withholding is the top marginal rate of 49 per cent, which is the primary reason you do not deal with anyone who cannot give you a tax invoice.

Withholding taxes are discussed in more detail in chapter 11, on employing staff.

Withholding taxes are paid on your quarterly BAS, or your monthly IAS if your withholding amounts exceed $25 000 per annum. They are the actual amounts withheld, not estimates, and are expenses deductible from your business income. Salary and wage tax instalment deductions are debited to the individual's wages account and will appear on their payslips and their annual payment summary.

Paying your tax bills (PAYG)

A Business Activity Statement, or BAS, is normally required each quarter. On your quarterly BAS you will pay:

▶ your actual net GST for the quarter

▶ if you have employees, the actual amount withheld as income tax payable from their wages

▶ your estimated income tax liability for the quarter (sole traders and companies)

▶ your FBT estimate for the quarter if your previous FBT annual payments exceeded $3000

▶ a number of specialty taxes such as wine equalisation, luxury car and fuel tax credits that are beyond the scope of this text.

You pay the total amount of all of these applicable taxes as one quarterly payment.

Each quarter you will be sent a pre-printed BAS with your name and address details already filled in. You simply complete the payment details and post it with your cheque or use one of the other payment options available. If you are not registered for the GST but are required to pay PAYG, then you will be sent a similar quarterly return but it will be called an Instalment Activity Statement (IAS) and it will not include the GST component.

When you lodge your annual income tax and fringe benefits return the Tax Office will estimate the amount of your tax liabilities for the next year. Each quarter it will send out a pre-printed BAS with the estimate already included. The first BAS will contain the options available, both for income tax and for the GST.

For income tax, payment may be based on either a fixed estimate or a percentage of annual turnover. It is recommended that you accept the Tax Office estimate method as this does not require you to complete your accounting procedures for the quarter before payment.

For the GST you also have three options:

▶ Each quarter you work out your GST liability and pay that amount. This method is used by the vast majority of GST-registered small businesses.

▶ You estimate your GST quarterly and report annually. But there are penalties for getting the estimate wrong, so why would you use this method?

▶ You pay the Tax Office estimate quarterly and report annually.

As there are significant penalties associated with the two estimate options, it is highly recommended that you calculate and pay your GST quarterly and be done with it! However, make sure you lodge your BAS within 14 days of the end of the quarter or again you will be penalised. We'll discuss this further in chapter 9.

Particular arrangements for each business structure

The above analysis is a *generalisation* of the procedures. Each class of business, whether sole trader, partnership or company, will have slightly different arrangements.

Individuals in business as sole traders

For an individual in business, the Tax Office will make no distinction between you and your business, but it is very unwise for *you* to fail to make this distinction. The best approach is to register a business name with the local state authority and then set up a business bank account in this name. Keep your business records completely separate from your personal account.

Before you can register a business name or set up a business bank account, however, you will need to obtain an Australian Business Number (ABN) and register for the GST, if applicable, and also PAYG, again if applicable.

The Tax Office we send you either a BAS or an IAS (depending on whether or not you register for the GST), and it will cover both your private and business income. If you receive a large amount of interest privately, the IAS will reflect this even though it is nothing to do with your business. Usually for small business in this category the IAS/BAS reflects your business earnings, but be aware that other amounts could be included.

In business as a partnership

For partnerships you will receive a BAS only if you register the partnership for the GST (the partnership must also register for an ABN and a TFN). The partnership does not pay any income tax and therefore the BAS will have a nil amount in the income tax box. Income tax is paid at partner level based on your proportion of the partnership income. Therefore you as an individual will also receive a quarterly IAS to account for your income tax on the partnership income.

For companies

You will register the company for an ABN and a TFN. A company pays GST, FBT and income tax, therefore it will get a quarterly BAS that will include the GST, income tax and withholding (PAYG) from staff wages.

Annual returns

There are a number of annual returns you may have to fill in. If you are an individual in business, then there is your annual income tax return. This is the same as any individual but with the addition of 'business items'. You will get a credit for the income tax paid on your quarterly BAS and either receive a refund or need to pay the difference.

If you are in partnership then you will need to fill in a partnership return. No tax is payable on this return. Its main purpose is to set out the percentage of the partnership income to be included in each individual partner's tax return. It is this amount of the partnership income, together with other untaxed amounts, that will form the estimate on the IAS that you, as an individual, will be required to pay each quarter. If the annual estimate is low enough, you may elect to make just one annual payment. The Tax Office will notify you if your estimated liability falls within this category.

If your business is a company, then the company must fill in an annual income tax return and pay 28.5 per cent of the taxable income (tax profit). The taxable income can then be passed on, along with the tax paid, to the shareholders in proportion to their holdings and returned on their individual tax returns. You must note this 'distribution' in your records and also keep a record of the taxable profit (income), income tax paid and distributions made. This is referred to as a *franking account*. Other annual returns required by a company include FBT (31 March) and ASIC (anniversary of date of registration).

Capital gains tax (CGT)

There is surprisingly little to say about small business and CGT. Capital gains tax applies when you sell an asset. You either make a gain or suffer a loss on the sale. The gain, minus any CGT losses for the year and any previous CGT losses, is included in your income.

For small business taxpayers, however, any asset that is subject to depreciation is not subject to capital gains tax. Therefore, the assets to which CGT may apply are very limited.

If you own shares or other investments through the business, then CGT may apply if you dispose of them. The 50 per cent general exception applies to individuals and partnerships, but not to companies as such.

There are also special concessions available for micro businesses, usually aimed at providing retirement income for the business owners. The concessions are, in summary:

▶ an additional 50 per cent reduction (over and above the general 50 per cent) if the asset sold is an *active business asset* (but not a depreciating asset)

▶ small business rollover defers the capital gain on a depreciating asset that is sold and replaced with a like asset

▶ a small business retirement exemption where the proceeds of the sale are paid into a superannuation fund (age 55 and $500 000 conditions apply)

▶ an exemption for business assets owned over 15 years when the business owner is over 55 and retiring.

Generally it is only on the sale of your business that these exemptions may apply.

Small businesses should be aware that you may still be eligible for the CGT concessions (if you have net assets of $6 million or less) and the FBT car parking exemption (if your total ordinary income plus statutory income is less than $10 million). This is more fully explained in chapters 6 and 7, which are devoted to the CGT and FBT taxes and how they apply to both micro and small businesses.

The golden rule is, if you sell an asset, apart from anything that is a depreciable asset or trading stock, then you should seek professional advice.

State-based taxation

All the taxes reviewed above are collected by the federal government. There is also a raft of state-based taxation regimes. The two that are most common are payroll tax and stamp duty. These differ from state to state, so we can make only a general comment on each.

Payroll tax

Payroll tax applies only to businesses with fairly large payrolls. Each state has a different threshold and taxing rate. For example, in NSW your payroll must exceed $750 000 before you are subject to the tax at a flat 5.45 per cent; in Queensland it is $1 100 000 and 4.75 per cent. Of course, these rates were current at the time of writing and are subject to change.

State duties (stamp duty)

State-based 'duties' apply to the value of contracts that pass legal ownership in certain specified goods or services, usually land (including leases and mortgages), motor vehicles, insurance and trusts, although each state authority has its own list of dutiable items and rates. Failure to pay these duties, evidenced in the past by the attachment of revenue stamps to the contract, makes the contract unenforceable at law.

Getting information

You should consult your own state tax authorities to determine if any state taxes and duties apply in your situation. Most of them have publications for small businesses operating within their state.

The business entry point 'Taxation' at www.business.gov.au has links to all state taxation offices.

Small business concessions

Small business tax concessions apply to micro businesses that have an 'aggregate' turnover of less than $2 million. There is no longer an asset test applying to these provisions, but you must actually be in business, not just in the start-up phase.

You do not have to notify the Tax Office if you wish to use these concessions, but you must note in your accounting records that this is what you are basing your tax calculations on. This would apply especially to the depreciation method you adopt. More on this topic later!

Your turnover is the total of all income made by the business from the provision of goods or services—your total sales, fees and commissions. By aggregate turnover the Tax Office means the total turnover of all your business ventures; this is proportioned for those businesses that have started partway through the year.

These 'concessions' are contingent on the following conditions:

▶ You must account for your income tax liability on a cash basis. This means you can also elect to treat your GST liability on a cash basis. (This book assumes that you have made that choice.) Small businesses in excess of $2 million in turnover must account for their income tax and GST liabilities on an accrual basis—that is, based on a legal liability rather than on a funds transfer.

▶ If you purchase any asset costing less than $1000, you can write it off as an immediate expense, a low-cost asset. Small businesses in excess of $2 million in turnover must account for assets that cost less than $1000 in a 'Low Value Pool' at a rate of 37.5 per cent per year. *Note:* This book reflects the current Liberal government's stated intention to reduce this low-cost asset concession from $5000 for cars and utes and $6500 for other assets, to under $1000. This was to be effective 1 January 2014, but is yet to be legislated. Please refer to my website www.tpabusiness.com.au for the latest on this change.

▶ All other assets generally have the one depreciation rate of 30 per cent. Small businesses in excess of $2 million in turnover must assess each asset, or class of assets, according to the asset's effective life.

▶ You do not have to account for stock variations provided they do not move by more than $5000 per year. Small businesses in excess of $2 million in turnover must account for the difference between the opening and closing stock levels for each income year.

▶ You do not have to account for any capital gains tax consequence of selling a depreciating asset. Other taxpayers must treat any private use component under the CGT rules.

▶ You can claim pre-paid expenses (up to 12 months ahead) as an immediate deduction. Small businesses in excess of $2 million in turnover must apportion pre-payments over the period to which they relate.

▶ You must account for any income received in advance when you receive it. Small businesses in excess of $2 million in turnover must apportion their income over the period to which it relates.

Private use of business assets

There is not a business owner in Australia who has not at some time used their company credit card for a private purchase or taken stock off the shelf for their own use. There is nothing illegal or wrong with this; in fact, it is common practice. It becomes a problem only if the private use is not handled correctly in the accounts, with the correct adjustments made to reflect the correct amounts of GST and income tax that you pay.

The other private use problem relates to employee 'perks'. How do we handle the company paying for an employee's golf club membership out of company funds?

One main area we will not address here is the private use issues with motor vehicles. This is a major topic in its own right, and I will leave the discussion of the private use of business motor vehicles and the FBT implications thereof to chapter 8.

First let's summarise how we deal with the private use issue before we look at the issue in more depth:

▶ If you spend business funds for private purposes, add them to your equity (drawings) account, including the private portion of the GST credit.

▶ If you are *really* using a business asset for private use — that is, your use is not *incidental* — then you can claim only the business use portion of the asset for GST and use the business portion for depreciation purposes.

▶ If you take stock off the shelf, adjust the inventory and GST against your drawings account at the cost of purchase, not the selling price.

▶ Business owners' private use is subject to FBT only if the business is an incorporated company (Pty Ltd); in other cases you are required to account for the private use as stated above.

▶ For employees, if you give them any private use of company assets, including paying for private expenses, then you are subject to FBT! Far better to give them an allowance or a reimbursement rather than run the risk of FBT.

What is 'private use'?

It is normal in a business enterprise for some of the business assets (such as motor vehicles or mobile phones) to be used partly for private purposes. It is also normal practice for the business to pay some of the owner's private accounts (for example the home telephone, electricity and newspapers).

How do we account for these expenses and how are they taxed?

This is a complex issue that is at the heart of most problems you will face in accounting for your business income and expenses. There are two classes of persons we need to discuss separately under this heading: these are the business owners and the employees of the business.

Private use by the business owners

Private use falls into two categories. You can use business funds to purchase private goods (to buy your morning newspaper, say), and you can use business assets for private purposes, such as the business computer your son uses to do his homework. It should be noted here that the term *owner* also includes your family members. In tax parlance, these are known as associates.

Owner's private expenses paid out of business funds

If you use business funds to make a purchase that is for private use, including assets for 100 per cent private use, you cannot claim the 'private portion' of the expense as an income tax deduction, nor can you claim a GST credit for the private portion. For example, Jenny has a hairdressing business and is registered for GST. She obtains her own personal hairdressing products (shampoos, brushes and so on) by making a separate order with her supplier. These acquisitions are all of a private nature and cannot be creditable acquisitions, and nor are they business expenses. These expenses would be debited against her drawings account at the cost of the goods to the business, not the selling price.

Owner's private use of assets, with the exception of cars, can be handled in a number of ways, but in this book it is treated as a shared resource, recording only the business portion into your accounts with the private portion being debited to the drawings (suspense) account. Chapter 4 discusses this in more detail.

Calculating the private use percentage (business use percentage in tax terms)

The Courts have decided a number of 'private use' cases, usually on their particular merits without stating a general principle. It is for you to decide what is private and what is business use, and usually it is not as easy as the above example.

Let us say that you run a small publishing business from your home. You buy a computer for this business. Being in your home it will probably be used for private purposes as well, but to what extent? Perhaps your son likes to play computer games and uses the computer for this purpose. Is this private use? The Tax Office would say definitely yes! I would say it depends...

If the computer is available at all times for business use — that is, he plays games only when the machine is not in use, and he is required to give up the machine at any time it is required for business, then I would call this is *incidental use*, not private use. There are no tax consequences of incidental use of business assets. If your son did his homework on the machine and gets preferential use between 6 pm and 9 pm each night, then this would be a private use and subject to tax treatment.

This is only the personal opinion of the author, but I believe that a *right to use* must be present before a private use component can be established — for example, a motor vehicle used to travel to and from work. The employee has a right to use, therefore this is a private use.

There are no legal rules that direct how you are to determine your private use percentage. Generally you should try to determine the private use by a direct calculation (number of hours used privately versus number of hours used for business purposes, or number of kilometres travelled for private purposes versus total kilometres). These calculations should be done over a test period, say six weeks, and the written (diary) results held as proof of your private use percentage. You can also attempt to estimate usage, such as percentage of floor area used, but the direct method is preferred.

Once established, the business use percentage for each asset is used to determine the proportion of the depreciation expense that you can claim as a business deduction and the amount of the GST credit you can claim on purchase or replacement.

Tax Office estimates

For some industries, the Tax Office has estimated the amount that it would be reasonable to include in your private income for goods taken from the trading stock of small businesses for use by the family.

As an example, a baker would include $1310 for each adult in the family and $655 for each child in their business income to account for the goods taken from inventory for private use. Other examples are included in table 5.1 (see p. 95).

To account for this private use you would make a journal entry, usually on an annual basis, deducting (Cr) the amounts from purchases and adding them (Dr) to your drawings account. *Note:* these estimates do not include GST.

You do not have to use these amounts, but if you decide to account for private use by another method, you must keep detailed records of any goods taken.

Drawings account (suspense account)

For companies, the balance of the drawings account (more correctly called a suspense account) should be converted into salary each quarter. For other business structures, such as individuals or partnerships, the owner's drawings account is offset with the business taxable income at year's end.

Accounting for private use

As an example, let us assume that you pay the household electricity account through the 'home-based' business cheque account. The business occupies 20 per cent of the property area, therefore the private use proportion is 80 per cent. The electricity account is $110, including $10 GST.

Only the business portion is claimable for both GST and income tax, therefore you would allocate the private portion to the drawings account:

Dr	Electricity	$20	business use proportion
Dr	GST account	$2	GST on business use proportion
Dr	Drawings	$88	Private use including GST
	Cr Bank		$110

On the other side of this example, if you pay the electricity account out of private funds then how do you claim the business portion? Again, it is against the drawings account:

Dr	Electricity	$20	business use proportion
Dr	GST account	$2	GST on business use proportion
	Cr Drawings	$22	Paid from private funds

If you are a sole trader, the drawings form part of the profit you made on the business; for partnerships they form part of the profit distribution; for companies they form part of the owner's salary. Please note that technically a private company (Pty Ltd) cannot have an owner's drawings account as the business is an entity unto itself, but in the small business world a drawings account is used as above. It is technically a suspense account to be cleared before year's end.

Note that the Tax Office uses an alternate term, the *business use percentage*. This is because the business use is deductible whereas the personal use is not. If one-third of an asset is for private use, then two-thirds is for business use. The tools on our website, www.tpabusiness.com.au, apply the term *business use* to be consistent with the Tax Office terminology.

Private use by your *employees*

The next set of problems concerns private expenditure of business funds or private use of business assets by employees. All employees' private use is handled under the fringe benefits tax rules *irrespective* of the business structure.

The main contenders here are motor vehicles, union fees, laptop computers, mobile phones, protective clothing (overalls), home phones and superannuation. I have deliberately mixed these up because the first thing to realise is that not all expenses are treated the same.

▶ As an employer you can provide your employees with one laptop computer each per year without the need to account for any private use of that item. In tax parlance, it is FBT exempt. Superannuation is also FBT exempt. There are no FBT tax implications of providing superannuation for your employees.

▶ If your employee would get a tax deduction if they paid for the item, then there is no FBT implication under the *otherwise deductible rule*—union fees fall within this category.

▶ If you provide items for which there is no private use—as in the case of protective clothing—then there are no FBT implications.

In all other cases you must account for the private use. Please refer to the section on fringe benefits tax that deals with this topic at some depth.

Bookkeeping and recording systems

If you are contemplating starting a business, then you must also consider the method you will adopt to account for your income and expenses. The days of the shoe box of receipts to be sorted by your accountant at year's end are well and truly over. Today each and every business, no matter how small, needs to use a computerised accounting system from day 1. You should also note that the Tax Office can fine you for failing to keep adequate records. Fortunately they must give you a warning for your first offence.

Computer systems

There are three levels of choices available to you: the basic cashbook systems (often a spread sheet adaptation); entry-level accounting systems such as MYOB or Quicken; and the more advanced systems such as Attaché or Sybiz.

As MYOB has over 70 per cent of the small business market, I would recommend that this be your starting point. The examples in this book are from MYOB Accounting. The availability of training by independent educators and TAFE is an added bonus. If your business is too complex for these entry-level systems, then there are over a hundred more advanced accounting packages to look at. Your accountant should have access to CPA Australia's annual accounting software guide, which lists all the most common accounting programs and their features.

If you have only one or two employees, the Tax Office website contains a basic salary calculator that you could use. It may save you the cost of an additional payroll package and the training involved with its use. Alternatively, both MYOB and Quicken have payroll add-ons.

In-house bookkeeper, contract bookkeeper or do your own thing?

In today's business world approximately one-third of all businesses fail within the first year. One reason for this is failure to keep control over their expenditure. You must take control of your own accounting. This does not mean that you can't seek assistance from bookkeeping services, but you must retain ultimate responsibility.

'Doing the books' involves a number of stages, including recording the income and expenses, the month-end processing, monthly and quarterly production of the tax and financial reports, and finally the annual processing and rollover. If the first element, the recording, is wrong then all other processes that depend on this will be incorrect.

You have three options to make sure that everything is correctly recorded:

▶ Do it yourself, with assistance from your own accountant or bookkeeper (now must be a Registered BAS Agent).

▶ Do the basic recording yourself and have someone, on a monthly or quarterly basis, double check your work and provide any advice needed.

▶ Employ a full bookkeeping service, either at your premises or as a remote data entry, to undertake the work.

Which option you choose really depends on the complexity of your business and the availability of advice. One point to keep in mind is that bookkeepers are now required to be registered with the Tax Office and therefore the costs associated with this kind of service are escalating. Doing your own books is the only sure way of keeping these costs under control.

With the appropriate assistance, you should not have any difficulty in recording your own accounting data, provided of course you are using a product such as MYOB and have undertaken the necessary training.

CHAPTER 2
Business structures

Key areas we will cover in this chapter

▶ Tax-effective business structures

▶ Sole trader

▶ Partnership

▶ Company Pty Ltd

▶ Trusts

▶ Family discretionary trusts

Defined terms we will introduce

TFN (tax file number): the number assigned by the Tax Office to your income tax return

ABN (Australian Business Number): the Tax Office–assigned number required by every business, mainly used for GST purposes

Sole trader: a person in business on their own

Partnership: two or more persons in business jointly

Company: an entity created by registering the business as a company with ASIC

Trust: a tax-effective business structure, usually assigning family members as beneficiaries

ASIC (Australian Securities and Investments Commission): Australia's corporate and financial services regulator

FBT (fringe benefits tax): a tax on the 'perks' given to employees or the private use of business assets by the business owners

A well-known Hollywood movie features an imprisoned banker. When he overhears the brutal chief guard complaining about his tax problems he breaks in: 'Do you trust your wife?' The reaction is predictably violent—until the guard listens to the advice the former banker has to offer.

Tax planning is all about spreading the tax burden around family members in order to utilise their lower tax rates. Australian personal tax rates are progressive: your first $18 200 is tax free, the next $18 000 is taxed at 19 per cent, and so on. The percentage you pay goes up with the taxable income you earn. If you can spread your business income around the family you can utilise this structure to your own benefit.

The downside is that your family members will effectively become your business partners, and this could have ramifications in the case of family breakdown. It should also be noted that this income will form the basis of the calculation of any tax or social security benefits the member may be entitled to and therefore could have an adverse impact on these benefits.

But first let us examine what strategies are available.

Tax-effective business structures

It is a basic accounting law that you and your business are two separate entities. You should never confuse your personal affairs with your business dealings. Rule 1 in business is that your business should have its own bank account, chequebook, credit cards and so on. By this I do not mean that you cannot use your business funds for private purposes, but that, when you do so, you should accurately record that fact. Keep them separate or suffer the consequences! If you don't keep separate and discrete business records, then your accountant will have a very difficult time separating your private affairs from your business affairs, and you will have to pay for him to do this. Also, the Tax Office itself requires that you are able to prove your business income and expenses, and there are penalties for failing to do so.

So what should your business look like? That depends very much on what your business is.

Sole trader—John Smith Lawn Mowing

An individual in business is called a sole trader. If it is just you in the business, there is no need to go further than setting yourself up as a sole trader. This is especially the case for contractors who earn their income from 'personal services'. Your business income will be declared in the business section of your personal tax return and you will not have a separate business tax return to complete, although you will register a separate ABN just for your business. This may sound confusing, but that is why it is important, as much as possible, to keep all your business dealings separate from your private affairs.

Partnership—John & Jane Smith trading as John's Lawn Mowing

Businesses that are operated by just one person are unusual; the most common business structure is husband and wife in business jointly. A partnership is the cheapest of all tax-effective structures to set up. It is constituted via a partnership agreement. This does not have to be a formal agreement; it does not even have to be in writing, but it is best to write a simple agreement in which you both consent to creating a partnership. The agreement will define the business that you are going to be in, agree what each of you is going to contribute to the partnership, and agree to a method of profit sharing and level of 'salary', if any, to be paid.

You will need to register the partnership wit the Tax Office and get a TFN and ABN for that business. A partnership has to file a tax return each year, but no tax is payable on that return. The income tax payable on the partnership income is paid by the individual partner on their share of the partnership profits and at their individual tax rate. The partnership tax return simply informs the Tax Office of the individual partner's share of the total partnership income. All of the partnership's taxable income must be 'distributed' (allocated) to the partners for income tax purposes.

Incorporated business—John & Jane Smith Pty Ltd trading as John's Lawn Mowing

If a business's name ends in Pty Ltd (MyCompany Pty Ltd), it signifies that it is registered with ASIC as a private company. 'Pty' stands for *proprietary* (or private), 'Ltd' indicates your liability is 'limited' by shares. These businesses are referred to in this book as companies.

Such a business structure is usually set up by your accountant. It will cost from $2000 to set up and anywhere between $1000 and $5000 a year in accounting fees. Being a business registered with the Australian Securities and Investments Commission requires that you also lodge an annual return with ASIC, which for private companies currently costs $220 and is not onerous to complete. ASIC posts a pre-filled form to you each year, on the anniversary date of registration, which you amend with any changes required and then return with the payment.

You can set up a company as just one person (a single director) or more than one person. It gives some protection in the event of bankruptcy, but this protection is continually being eroded by the Courts. Increasingly owners (directors) are being held personally liable for the actions of private companies.

The main benefit is that the Tax Office will accept a proprietary company as a business with little question. The tax rate is 28.5 per cent flat, compared to the maximum of 49 per cent for an individual, and there is no penalty for holding the business earnings within the business. It can employ you and your spouse on wages in order to maximise the lower tax rates and you can pay a number of personal expenses through the business.

The downside is the administration cost and the fact that fringe benefits taxes usually apply to businesses with personal dealings with the owners and that you lose the benefit of the 50 per cent capital gains tax reduction available to individuals.

The company will need to apply to the Tax Office for an ABN and a TFN and to file a tax return each year on which it will pay a 28.5 per cent tax on profits. The profits can be distributed to the shareholders (owners), with the tax paid used as a credit against your individual income.

Companies are quite complex tax structures, but the basic bookkeeping requirements are the same for all businesses. It is only the profits distribution that is different, so if you keep a good set of books your tax accountant's fees will be kept to a minimum.

Trusts — John & Jane Smith Pty Ltd as trustee for MyFamily Trust trading as John's Lawn Mowing

Every reasonably sized business in Australia has been traditionally operated through a family discretionary trust with a corporate trustee. If you think that sounds complex, it is! The more complex, the more expensive, but the family trust structure does have its place in the corporate world.

Trusts are in many ways the most complex method of setting up your business structure, and arguably the cost may not match the benefits. In the above example the 'trustee' is a company, John & Jane Smith Pty Ltd trust, and the 'business' is the trust. Your business would have to be very profitable to justify the cost but it can in some instances be a very good, tax-effective structure.

So exactly what is a trust?

Trusts certainly have a place, primarily for the protection of assets in the case of a business bankruptcy or marriage breakdown, for example. Once your business is established and making money, then it might be time to ask your accountant about the benefits and costs of operating in this manner.

The origin of trusts is lost in antiquity, but the story that most appeals is that they began in England during the reign of Henry VIII, a period when England was almost continually at war with France. This war came very close to bankrupting the Crown. In response Henry introduced a form of death duties. The nobility of the time came up with a novel scheme that would protect them from this impost — and so the first tax planning scheme was born.

The scheme involved the landed gentry 'gifting' the land to the Church on the basis that the Church would hold that land 'in trust' for the benefit of the gentleman's descendants. Some of those descendants, primarily the eldest son, would have full rights to the estate. Others, such as the surviving spouse or the other siblings, would have rights to part of the income from the estates.

The modern-day family trust is just such a tax planning device. It attempts to divert income from the taxpayer on whom the initial obligation rests to other family members who may be in a better tax position. Money need not change hands, only the tax obligation. If this sounds a bit 'suspect', then you understand the basis of the Tax Office's position that such trusts are in fact tax minimisation schemes.

That is not to say that trusts do not have a rightful place. They do in the case of deceased estates, compensation payments, bankruptcy protection and divorce. But generally they are used for tax minimisation purposes.

Basically a trust is made up of three parties. The *settlor* gifts the property to a *trustee*, who holds the trust estate for the benefit of the *beneficiaries*.

From a taxation perspective you will need to engage a tax accountant to guide you through this maze. Today's approach by the Tax Office is to view trusts as a conduit through which the tax obligation passes into the hands of the beneficiaries. There are penalties if funds are not distributed to the beneficiaries, or are distributed incorrectly or inappropriately.

Trusts are the most complex of all business structures, so they are also the most expensive to set up and maintain. Only a business that is making a substantial profit would seek this type of structure; on the other hand, it is the most tax-effective method of reducing your overall tax liability.

One additional word of warning: a trust distribution will be classed as income to the beneficiary whether or not they actually received the money into their account. As income, it will be included in all income tests for social security and other benefits and obligations such as child maintenance.

How much tax does each structure incur?

Let us assume that your business makes a profit of $100 000:

▶ As a sole trader you would pay $24 950.

▶ As a husband-and-wife partnership you would each pay $7800, for a total of $15 600.

▶ As a company you would pay $28 500, which is then distributed to the shareholders, you and your wife, and included in your own tax return with a credit for tax paid—arguably the same end result as in a partnership.

► As a trust with five 'adult' family members, each would pay $342, for a total of $1710.

This comparison makes it obvious that a partnership is the preferred tax structure for small businesses, but once your business becomes profitable to the extent that the tax savings will more than offset the cost, then a family trust with a corporate trustee is the most tax-effective structure. Most small businesses currently operate through a trust.

Women rule!

The example of John Smith Lawn Mowing reflects the traditional small business arrangement of a working dad/home mum family. Today, however, more than 70 per cent of all small businesses are started by women, a large proportion as home-based businesses, and many of which of outgrow the kitchen, home office or garage to become sizable businesses in their own right. For inspiration, read the story on a Carman's cereal box. Another example is iiNet, which started in a family garage and is now a multi-million-dollar business.

The truth is you have to protect your interest in this area irrespective of whether you are male or female, husband or wife, or doing it all alone. The above advice applies equally to everyone, to the extent that the law permits.

Tax rules

Australian tax law contains rules on how an individual resident taxpayer will determine their taxable income. These rules are more or less consistent with the accounting standards we use to determine a small business's profit. Tax law also contains rules for partnerships, companies and trusts. However, these rules relate to how the taxable income is to be taxed and distributed (or distributed and taxed, depending on the structure), not how to determine the taxable income in the first instance.

Therefore the way in which tax law can be viewed is that once you have determined your taxable income as a resident individual, you can apply the tax rules that relate to your specific entity to determine who bears the tax burden—yourself as an individual, your partners, shareholders or beneficiaries—and as a consequence, just how much your business endeavours will be taxed. This is generally referred to as *tax planning* or *tax minimisation*.

But unfortunately that is not the end of the story. Tax law in this country is a political instrument—that is, each new government, when it wins power, seeks to modify the tax regime to suit its own political agenda. For this reason you have to be mindful of all of the exemptions and concessions that modify what would be normal accounting practice, both in the calculation of your taxable income and in its distribution to the business owners, partners or beneficiaries, as the case may be. We will cover many of these exemptions and concessions in the next chapter, on taxable income.

Family discretionary trusts

The family discretionary trust is used by the majority of small businesses in Australia as a most effective tax structure. However, before we go any further I must point out that:

▶ a trust will affect the amount of tax you pay on your income but will have no effect on your GST or FBT liabilities

▶ irrespective of the tax structure you decide upon, the bookkeeping procedures that you adopt up to the point of calculating your taxable income (profit) will be identical.

To explain how a trust works, I will use an example. Let us assume that you, Mr Jones, are in business as a sole trader under the name of MyBusiness and that your business is now doing very well, but that your income tax bill is now of concern. Your accountant suggests that you put your business assets into a trust and distribute your taxable income among your family members, utilising their tax-free thresholds.

We will now look at how that works, but first I must point out that this is a legal 'sleight of hand'. What I am going to describe is a legal fiction and makes no practical sense whatsoever. You just have to go with it!

So first we need a trust deed. Your accountant will draw up a document that creates the trust and nominates you as the settlor—that is, you will settle on to this trust all of your business assets. The beneficiaries of the trust are all your family members within three generations of yourself, from your grandparents through to your grandchildren.

Now you will need someone to administer the trust. This person is called a trustee. You could be nominated as the trustee but that would make you legally responsible. Better to hide behind a company structure, so we create a private company called by your business name MyBusiness Pty Ltd and nominate you as the sole director of this company. The full name of the trustee company is now 'MyBusiness Pty Ltd as Trustee for the Jones Family trust'.

So far it's just a lot of legal mumbo jumbo and you are out of pocket by anything up to $10 000.

You carry on with your business as normal and at the end of the year calculate your profit as usual. You now revisit your accountant in order to calculate your income tax liability.

What we have to do now is called a trust distribution, and this is where it gets interesting. A family discretionary trust is called 'discretionary' because you, as the effective trustee, have the discretion to allocate your business income to any member of your family you wish in order to reduce your tax liability. You will notice that I used the word 'allocate', not 'pay'. The business income is allocated around the family members for the purpose of income tax calculation, but the actual funds stay in the business to be used as you see fit.

Sounds too good to be true? Well it is in the sense that the accounts in your business now will show loans from your family members to the extent that they have been allocated the business income. Think of it as paying your family members the business income with one hand and taking it back as a loan to the business with the other. As the family member now has loan funds with the business, they are legally entitled to demand payment of those funds; in legal terms it's called a *present entitlement*.

The upshot is that you must ensure that all the family members are aware that you are using their underutilised tax position for the benefit of the business and that they agree not to pursue the money. The most famous case involving a family trust dispute in Australia in recent years involved the mining magnate Gina Rinehart in just these circumstances, with two of her children demanding payment of their 'entitlement' and the trustee challenging their claim.

So having settled that, we can now move into the legal nightmare that is a trust distribution, but first there are a two interrelated concepts that must be understood:

► *Income streaming.* Income to a trust retains its nature when distributed to the beneficiaries. For example, a capital gain to the business can be distributed as a capital gain to the beneficiaries. A dividend with franked credits attached can be distributed as a dividend and the franked credits used by the beneficiary to offset other income. This situation is the exact opposite of a company where all income becomes dividend income for distribution irrespective of its original nature.

So our first step is to examine the income and expenses of all of your potential beneficiaries, three generations either side of you, and see who would most benefit from income streaming. For example, if the business has a capital gain, is there a beneficiary who has a carry forward capital loss? If the business has received franked dividends, which beneficiary would most benefit from those franking credits?

► *The effect of an income distribution on the beneficiary.* Although a beneficiary is allocated only the income and does not actually receive the cash, the allocated income will be classed as income for all purposes including the income tests under the *Social Security Act* and child maintenance. Therefore you as trustee must have a very intimate knowledge of all of your potential beneficiary's financial affairs.

The knowledge you require to make a successful family distribution may seem all but unattainable, which is why it is normal practice for your accountant to advise you in these matters. However, in order to gain the knowledge required to make these calculations your accountant must be responsible for all of your family tax matters, including the calculation of your trust income, the trust tax return, the trustee company tax return (if required) and the individual tax returns of every member of your family who may be considered as a beneficiary to whom part of the trust income may be distributed. The cost to the business of running under a family trust arrangement is therefore very high. The real question is, are the savings made in tax in excess of the accountancy fees required to administer the trust? All too often the answer is no!

Now that your accountant has set up the distribution schedule you will review it and sign it as trustee, making the nominated beneficiaries 'presently entitled' to the trust distribution and therefore liable for the tax payable on their share of the trust income.

This has been a fairly basic overview of a very complex issue. To run a family trust you must have the professional assistance of your tax accountant. It is for this reason that many small business owners are now questioning the cost versus benefit of operating through this type of vehicle and are starting to turn back to the private company as the preferred structure.

Unit trusts

It is worth noting the distinction between a unit trust and a discretionary trust.

A unit trust is one in which all the beneficiaries are allocated units in the trust, which under the trust deed will have a fixed entitlement to the income and the capital of the trust. There can be different classes of units with differing entitlements, but all of the units will have a fixed entitlement of a predetermined class of income and capital. Once the income of the trust has been determined and declared, each unit beneficiary will automatically have a right to their individual portions of the trust income and capital according to the units' rights under the trust deed. This is completely different from the discretionary trust, where the trustee is able to stream income and capital to various beneficiaries as they see fit, and can do so differently from year to year. In a unit trust the distribution is fixed for each beneficiary and for all time, or until such time as the trust deed is legally modified.

Unit trusts are a popular way of protecting your investment in trusts involving non-family members or investments of property where each member makes a fixed contribution and the unit acknowledges that contribution percentage. For example, a brother and sister buy a property on the basis that each contributes 50 per cent of the capital, but the sister manages the property in return for a two-thirds share in the profits. The individual units could then be structured to give each a 50/50 split of the capital of the trust and a one-third to two-thirds split of the income.

Trusts and tax law

I should emphasise that I am talking about trusts in a fairly limited sense — that is, as a tax-effective business structure. Testamentary trusts are what we all call our 'last will and testament', and other types of trusts can be set up for passive investments. These types of structures are outside the scope of this small business text.

Penalties

When you make a distribution of taxable income in the case of a trust set up as a business structure, you should be aware that penalties apply to any amount of your taxable income that has not been distributed. The law intends that all of the trust's income should be distributed to its beneficiaries and will tax the trustee on any amount not so distributed at the top marginal rate for an individual plus the Medicare levy. This is the case even if the trustee is a company. For this reason the trust deed usually includes a 'default beneficiary' who will be automatically allocated any residual income that has, for one reason or another, not been allocated to a nominated beneficiary.

In addition to the above, if you set up a family trust by making a family trust election, then you are prevented by tax law from distributing any trust income outside of your family members. The trustee will be taxed on any income distributed to non-family members at the top marginal rate (plus Medicare levy).

Also, should you make a distribution of trust income to any beneficiary with a legal disability, such as an individual under 18 years of age, an undischarged bankrupt or a mentally incapacitated person, then again the trustee will be subject to tax on that distribution — in this case as if the income was the income of an individual taxpayer without any allowable deductions.

The trust deed

Tax law is heavily reliant upon the terms of the trust deed and will not allow any amount to be distributed to a beneficiary where that beneficiary is not entitled to that income under the terms of the trust deed.

Basically the trust deed must cover the distribution of the income of the business but explicitly state who is entitled to a trust distribution of income and further the types of income that can be distributed, especially in regard to interest, dividends and capital gains. This is to cover the concept of income streaming, as discussed previously.

Also, the trust deed must explicitly cover who will be entitled to the 'corpus' of the trust, which is in effect the capital upon which your business is based, especially in the case of the sale of the business or the business assets. Who will be entitled to those funds and in what circumstances? Capital gains need to be also covered under this heading as a capital gain can be considered as part of the corpus of the estate, whereas for tax purposes it is treated as income to the estate.

Unpaid present entitlements

When you sign the distribution schedule you are making a determination as trustee as to who is entitled to what share of the trust income. The nominated beneficiaries are now said to be presently entitled to that distributed amount. I have also noted that in a family trust situation the present entitlement of the individual family member is usually satisfied by creating a loan account (usually an equity account) in the books of the business that hold the amount of business income they have been allocated for tax purposes.

However, if one of your beneficiaries happened to be an 'associated' private company—that is, one held by you or a close family relative—then any amount you allocate to that company would actually have to be paid in cash or, again, tax penalties would follow.

Family discretionary trusts are discussed further in chapter 12. For more information on the issue of family trusts, please refer to the book I co-authored with N.E. Renton, *Family Trusts*, fifth edition, published by Wiley Australia.

My recommendation

The most effective structure to start any business is the partnership. This allows you to share the income with your spouse. You can set up a partnership in a fairly informal way and handle most, if not all, of the legal and tax technicalities yourself. When your partnership starts to outgrow itself, then you can convert to the more complex structures of a private company or perhaps a family trust.

The basic problem with a partnership is that you are 'severally and jointly' liable for your own actions and the actions of your partner. With husband and wife this is usually not an issue, but between friends and colleagues it can cause major problems.

If you feel you need to protect yourself—for example, you give advice for which you may be held accountable—then either a company structure or a trust structure with a corporate trustee may be more suitable. It will also afford some relief in the case of bankruptcy, divorce or other adverse circumstance.

You should seek the advice of a professional before settling on any one particular business structure, however, and ensure that the advice you receive includes a comprehensive cost–benefit analysis of the various options available to you.

CHAPTER 3

Taxable income

Key areas we will cover in this chapter

▶ Assessable income

▶ Allowable deductions

▶ Cash accounting

Defined terms we will introduce

Tax Act: the *Income Tax Assessment Act 1936* and the *Income Tax Assessment Act 1997,* which have to be read as one

Assessable income: your business income from all sources

Allowable deductions: your business expenses that the Tax Act allows you to deduct from the assessable income

De minimis rule: the principle that the law does not concern itself with trifles!

Taxable income: the amount on which you pay tax

The tax equation: taxable income = assessable income − allowable deductions

For the purpose of this discussion we will assume that you are in business (that is, we are discussing tax matters of a business rather than personal tax matters as an individual), and that you are a tax resident of Australia (that is, you are a permanent Australian resident, not a temporary resident or a branch of an overseas enterprise). You pay income tax on your taxable income. Taxable income is a figure calculated from your assessable income less your allowable deductions. Once you have determined your taxable income you can then apply the tax rate to that figure in order to calculate your gross tax payable, from which you deduct any tax offsets to determine the actual amount of tax payable.

The above sounds quite complex, and it is, but we can break it down into manageable segments to make sense of it.

Assessable income

The Tax Act states that taxable income is income according to normal concepts; however, it then further qualifies this to mean income derived (that is, obtained, got or acquired) either directly or indirectly from all sources whether in or outside of Australia. This is a very broad definition, but in normal business practice it simply means what you would normally consider as income to the business.

In addition, the Tax Act also defines certain income items as income, whether or not you consider them to be income according to normal concepts such as bounty or subsidy payments. Other statutory items include interest, dividends and royalties.

In some cases income can also be exempt, such as income derived by charities. However, exempt income is taken into account when determining an entity's loss position so a further category has also been included in the Act, and that is 'non-assessable non-exempt' income, which basically means it is not included for any purpose. The prime example of this is payments you receive by way of an amount of GST included in the goods or services that you sell. In the case of the GST component, it is stripped off and credited to the GST account, entirely separate from the income component.

It should be noted that income does not have to be in the form of money. It can be a benefit or offset that you receive, such as in a barter agreement. And further, income does not include windfall gains such as a lottery win and does not include amounts of capital such as the sale of a capital asset, but it does include income you may receive from illegal activities such as bribes.

As a general rule, compensation payments can also be income in that they are taxed under the same principles on which the item the compensation payment replaces was to be taxed. Therefore compensation for loss of income is income, as in the case of compensation for loss of profits from trading stock or loss of contract.

Foreign exchange gains or losses are handled separately from the general rules and are usually offset against the value of the item, goods or service from which the gain or loss was derived. Essentially the item is adjusted to its 'money price paid', to quote the Australian Customs definition of the value of imported goods.

Allowable deductions

Allowable deductions are amounts that you can deduct from your assessable income in order to calculate your taxable income. In accounting terms they are your *business expenses*.

The Tax Act states that a taxpayer can deduct from their assessable income any loss or outgoing to the extent that it is necessarily incurred to carry on a business for the purpose of gaining or producing the taxpayer's assessable income. But the loss or outgoing cannot be of a capital or domestic nature, incurred to produce exempt income or prevented from being a deduction by a specific provision of the Act.

In English, you can deduct the business portion of an expense (in the accounting sense) only where you are in business with the intention of making a profit. You should note that you must be 'in business'. Expenses incurred before you commence your business are not normally a tax deduction but are referred to as 'establishment costs' and are handled as a capital allowance, which we will discuss later. Also, expenses incurred in a 'hobby' business that are entered into without profit being the prime motive may not be a deductible expense. Refer to our discussion on 'Am I in business?' in chapter 1 for a more complete explanation of this concept.

Providing that you are in business with the intention of making a profit, your expenses do not have to be justified to the Tax Office. In tax terms they do not have to be a commercially reasonable amount. The High Court has ruled that 'it is not for the Court or the Commissioner to say how much a taxpayer ought to spend in obtaining his income, but only how much he has spent'. A legitimate business expense is not excluded just because you made a bad choice.

However, any expense you incur must relate to your income generation; in tax terms there must always be a nexus between the outgoing and the assessable income. Expenses structured to obtain a tax benefit are normally not allowable, nor are artificial schemes whose main intent is a tax benefit rather than a true business-related outgoing.

Specific exclusions

Some business expenses are specifically excluded from your tax calculations even though you may have included them in your expenses for accounting purposes. Examples of such expenditure are:

▶ penalties from breaches of the law, such as speeding or parking fines

▶ provision for long service leave, annual leave and sick leave; these are deductible only when actually paid

▶ expenses in relation to relatives (spouses in particular) accompanying you on a business trip

▶ expenses in relation to illegal activities

▶ membership of social clubs, such as a golf club

▶ entertainment expenses

▶ the provision of non-compulsory uniforms not listed in the Register of Approved Occupational Clothing; note this does not include protective clothing, which is deductible

▶ car parking for over four hours where the car was used just to travel from home to work.

You should note that if the excluded expense is subject to FBT then it may be deducted and the FBT paid on the outlay.

Specifically allowable deductions

Some deductible expenses are stated specifically in the tax law, either in the statute itself or as case law:

▶ *Repairs*: These costs are deductible to the extent that they return the item to its original state. Improvements are not deductible. This is covered in more detail during our discussion of capital allowances.

▶ *Bad debts*: These are deductible only when an actual debt has gone bad and is no longer recoverable. Provisions or estimates for bad debts are not deductible.

▶ *Managing your tax affairs*: This includes expenses incurred for your income tax preparation, seeking tax advice and attending tax audit meetings.

▶ *Preparation, registration, stamping of a lease*: These are in regard to the business property.

▶ *Borrowing expenses*: Where the principal borrowed is used to produce assessable income, to the extent that the monies are used for private purposes they are excluded.

▶ *Discharge of a mortgage*: If you mortgage property (such as your home) to secure a loan, and use the monies for business purposes, then the cost of discharging the mortgage is deductible to the extent that the borrowed monies were used for business purposes.

▶ *Terminating a lease*: To the extent that the leased property or licence was used for business purposes, you can deduct 20 per cent of the cost per year over a five-year period.

▶ *Travel between workplaces*: Travel between work and home is not an allowable deduction, but once at work, travel to another place of work, perhaps a second job, is an allowable deduction.

▶ *Amounts paid on behalf of employees to a complying superannuation fund*: However, the deduction is limited to amounts actually paid, not just accrued. The annual 'cap' limitations do not affect the employer's ability to deduct the amount, only the employee's tax position.

▶ *Deductions for business owners (self-employed)*: These deductions are allowable to the extent that they do not put the business into a loss situation.

The above list is just a brief summary of the legal position but provides a good practical overview.

Limitations to deductions

A number of limitations to deductions to expenditure would, under accounting rules, be considered a legitimate business expense. We have alluded to some of these already, such as entertainment expenses and the provision of employee clothing, but there are five areas that I would like to cover in more detail:

▶ prepaid expenditure

▶ losses for non-commercial activities

▶ substantiation

▶ payments to associated persons and relatives

▶ salary and wages.

Prepaid expenditure

The general tax rule that applies is similar to the accounting rules for end-of-year expenditure in that you must apportion such expenditure such that only amounts that relate to the current tax year are included as a deduction this year, and amounts that relate to next year are carried over to next year. This is standard accounting practice and is based on the days covered. A payment of an insurance bill of $1500 on 15 May would be apportioned $189 for this year and $1311 for next.

		30/06/14	30/06/15
15/05/14	$1500	$189	$1311

However, there are a few exceptions to this rule that apply to all business taxpayers. You can deduct amounts in the year in which they were paid:

▶ if the amount concerned is less than $1000; then it is deductible in the year it was incurred (a *de minimis* rule similar to one you would use for your accounting end-of-year adjustments)

▶ if the amount is required to be paid by court order or government legislation, or

▶ if the payment was under contract for service (payments of salary or wages).

There is also a specific deduction allowed businesses that are entitled to use the small business tax concessions. In addition to the above, micro businesses, those with under $2 million in turnover, can deduct a prepaid expense incurred in the normal course of business, provided the prepayment does not exceed 12 months; that is, micro businesses do not have to apportion their prepaid expenses but can claim them outright.

Losses for non-commercial activities

This restriction applies only to small businesses with an 'adjusted' taxable income (taxable income plus reportable superannuation contributions, reportable fringe benefits and net investment losses) less than $250 000 per year. If your business falls into this category and you make a tax loss — that is, your allowable deductions exceed your *assessable income* — then you may not be able to claim that loss against other income.

However, this restriction does not apply if:

▶ your assessable income is greater than $50 000

▶ your business has produced a profit (positive taxable income) in three of the last five years

▶ the real property that you use in your business exceeds $500 000, or

▶ the value of other assets used in the business, not including vehicles, exceeds $100 000.

This rule is aimed at hobby businesses or start-ups where you make a loss. In these cases the loss is carried forward and can be deducted against future profits.

Substantiation

The golden rule is simple: if you expend more than $10 on any business-related item or activity, then your expense must be supported by written evidence from your supplier such as an invoice. You can also use a credit card statement or similar document, and if that document does not actually identify the item you can write it in.

You must retain the evidence for your claim for at least five years. Archiving of business records is a normal part of your annual cycle and should be done on a regular basis. The five-year rule in tax is a common requirement and should be adhered to for all your records whether or not they have a direct bearing on your tax position.

If you claim an expense without supporting documentation, then the deduction may be disallowed and a fine of 25 per cent of the tax claimed imposed. However, there are some exclusions to this rule for individual taxpayers, such as if the total of all your work-related expenses does not exceed $300 or your laundry expenses do not exceed $150 in total.

Substantiation for car expenditure is another area that is covered by its own rules and will be discussed in chapter 8.

Payments to associated persons and relatives

If you deal with a relative in the normal business sense, then there is not a problem. The problem can arise where you 'pay' your spouse for services performed. If your partner works for your business away from home, then a 'commercial standards' text applies. Would you pay an unrelated employee the same? If your partner works from home, then it is a question of the service performed and the time spent on the activity.

If you compensate your partner for work performed to the same extent that you would be willing to pay someone 'at arm's length' to do the same, then there is not a problem. The problem arises only with excessive payments, especially tax-effective payments to utilise the spouse's tax-free threshold, for example.

Salary and wages

Before you employ anyone, including yourself if your business is a company, you should register with the ATO as an employer. You forward the tax withheld from your employee's wages in your quarterly IAS/BAS. The quarterly BAS will still be sent to you by the Tax Office every quarter. The IAS contains just the withholding fields, the BAS all fields including income tax and GST if applicable. If your annual withholding amount exceeds $25 000, then an IAS will be sent to you *each month* to record and pay the withholding tax you have deducted from your employees for the month.

When calculating wages you will need to answer the following questions:

▶ What is the gross pay for the period including overtime and penalties?

▶ Are there any allowances payable for the period and are they taxable?

▶ Does your employee salary sacrifice their superannuation?

▶ Does the employee claim the tax-free threshold? (You can only claim this once so if your employee works for you as a second job they may not be entitled to this threshold.)

▶ Does your employee have a HECS/HELP (university) debt?

▶ Does your employee wish to have additional tax taken out of their wages?

▶ Can your employee claim a rebate, such as a zone rebate?

You can pay your employee weekly, fortnightly or monthly but you must make the superannuation guarantee payments (for employees earning over $450 per month, this is discussed further in chapter 11) at least quarterly. You must also inform your employee in writing when you pay it and the amount. The income tax you deduct from your employee wages must be paid on either the quarterly BAS or the monthly IAS as appropriate.

You can deduct from your taxable income the salary and wages and all of the on-costs such as superannuation guarantee and employee withholding tax, but you can only deduct these amounts when you actually pay them. You cannot deduct amounts you set aside (make a provision for) in regard to holiday, and sick or long service leave, unlike in accounting where such amounts are expensed at the time the provision is made. Such amounts can be a tax deduction only when you actually pay them.

One exception to this is the income tax you have withheld from employees' wages and the superannuation charge on the wages. For the last payments in the tax year, you can account for these when you pay the wages themselves rather than when they actually fall due in the next tax year.

Owner's salaries are a little more complex. If you have structured your business as a company, then it is considered to be a separate legal entity and can employ you irrespective of the fact that you are the business owner. In this case your wages can be treated just like any other employee's.

In the case of a business structured as a sole proprietor or partnership, the business is not a separate legal entity; rather, legally you are the business and at law you cannot employ yourself. Any wages you pay yourself are simply drawings from the business in lieu of a profit distribution. The income that you include in your tax return is the assessable income of the business, or in the case of a partnership your portion of the assessable income. A trust is similar to a partnership in that you include in your income tax return your income from the trust as a beneficiary. Whether or not you can be employed by the trust depends on the legal status of the trustee. If you as an individual are the trustee then the answer is no, but if the trustee is a company then the answer is yes.

The complexities of payroll are dealt with at length in my book *Learn Small Business Accounting in 7 Days* (published by Wiley Australia).

Cash versus accrual accounting

The standard method of accounting used in Australian businesses (indeed worldwide under the International Financial Reporting Standards) is what is termed *accrual accounting*. Accrual accounting means you accrue (or record) your income when you have a legal right to be paid and conversely you record your expenses when you have a legal obligation to pay. It should be noted that the term 'legal' is used very loosely in this context and perhaps the word 'right' or 'obligation' would be better.

As an example of an accrual system, if I sell goods on credit terms on 29 June with a 60 days settlement period, that sale is included in my sales for 29 June and in this year's taxable income even though I will not be paid for another two months. Conversely, if I receive an invoice for an electricity account on 29 June I include that account in my expenses for the year, even if the payment date is not until mid July.

Under *cash accounting* you record your income and expense items only when you actually settle the account. Our sales would not be included until they were settled, but neither would the electricity account be included until it was paid.

Under accrual accounting you can have bad debts because your income is recorded on credit sale, and if that account is not satisfied then you have to offset the sales revenue with a bad debt expense.

Under cash accounting you may still legally incur bad debts but as you haven't recorded the income from the sale there is no need to adjust your accounting records for the bad debt.

You should also note that I have been talking only about income and expense items, not assets and liabilities. For the purposes of accounting and income tax the purchase of assets and the recording of liabilities are not affected by the use of cash versus accrual accounting.

However, under the GST rules all transactions with a GST component are recorded under either a cash or an accruals regime. As an example, if I purchase an asset, when I record that purchase I also record the GST component. But under the cash rules I can claim the GST outlay only when I settle the account, or under the accrual rules when ownership passes. And for income tax purposes I can claim the depreciation expense only when the asset is installed ready for use, irrespective of whether I have paid for it.

In our discussion of cash versus accruals we should be aware that cash is not always cash and accrual not always accrual. One of the tax concessions available to small business is the ability to use cash accounting for both income tax and GST purposes. However, cash accounting for the GST is not the same as cash accounting for income tax.

Under the income tax rules some items are recorded when the cash is received/paid whether or not you normally use cash or accrual accounting. These items include:

▶ salary and wages and on-costs such as superannuation guarantee payments

▶ interest, dividends and royalties where they are not part of your principal business activities.

Cash accounting

We have to be very careful with this term as there is in reality no actual definition of cash accounting. In the income tax world, cash accounting only refers to your income and expenses, and by extension your debtors and creditors. It has no effect on the manner in which you deal with asset purchases and as a consequence your depreciation deduction calculations or balancing adjustments upon disposal. For the purposes of the GST it covers all creditable acquisitions and disposals irrespective of their type.

Income

Under accrual accounting, you account for your income when the obligation to pay has been raised, usually on issue of the invoice. The timing of the settlement of the invoice has no bearing on the tax implications of the transaction, both under GST and income tax rules.

Under cash accounting, you account for your income when you actually receive the money, not when you sell the goods or perform the service. This distinction has no bearing on cash sales where the provision of the goods and payment occur at the same time, but it has some interesting complications for goods sold on credit (such as net 30 days) or a service performed, billed but not yet settled. In these cases you account for the income only when the account is actually paid.

If you run a small shop, your income is the daily takings. That is, you deduct the float from the takings, leaving the float in the till tray, and then reconcile the actual cash to the till receipt, sometimes called the 'Z' total. You then bank the day's takings. The income is recorded as cash sales. You must make sure that your daily sales reflect actual sales from your till receipt. If you take funds from the till then the banking must account for this, with the sales being the till receipt, the bank being the cash deposited and your drawings account reflecting the difference. If you do not do this correctly it is highly likely that your income according to your BAS and your income according to your income tax return will not tally, which will result in an ATO query—and we don't need that!

Issuing accounts

If your business is one in which you issue accounts, then you must always issue a tax invoice quoting your ABN number. If you do not, your client will be required to deduct 49 per cent of the payment and send that to the Tax Office as withholding tax. If you are registered for the GST the invoice should also include the amount of the GST. This can be as part of the cost structure or as a note on the bottom of the invoice. The GST is 10 per cent of the invoice price, not including the GST—that is, 1/11th of the total invoice price.

Handling the GST on sales

If you are registered for the GST you include the actual 'net' sale amount in your income and the GST component is credited to the GST collected account. Computerised accounting systems handle this automatically through the receipts module.

The 'stripping off' of the GST amounts can cause some concern in some industries that have both taxable and non-taxable supplies, such as the local deli. The Tax Office has issued some short-cut guidelines for these businesses. Please refer to the section on special rules for food retailers in chapter 9 for further details.

A note on GST: if you are registered for GST, then you must remit 1/11th of your sales to the Tax Office in settlement of your GST liability (less your GST credits). 'Forgetting' to include the GST in your sales calculation makes no difference. The GST is 1/11th of your sales value, not something you 'add on'.

Prepayments

If you receive income in the form of a prepayment, it is normal practice to class the income as a liability—that is, money owing to your client until you provide the service—and then journalising the amount to income only as the service is provided. The GST is credited and an income tax liability raised when the service is provided and the payment becomes unconditional.

Under cash accounting the GST payment and income tax liability is raised on receipt of the payment even though it is just a down payment conditional upon the provision of a future service. In some ways this 'concession' works against small business taxpayers.

Expenses

Under accrual accounting you account for an expense when it falls due, not when payment is made. Under cash accounting you account for your expenses when you actually pay the money. The difference between your income and your expenses for the year is your profit.

Your income tax liability is based on the difference between your assessable income and your allowable deductions. Most small businesses keep their records primarily to satisfy the tax man, therefore the accounting profit and the taxable income are usually the same.

Types of expenses

For income tax purposes, the cash basis relates only to your income and expense items, not to the purchase of assets and so on. The GST legislation makes no such distinction. This can lead to some interesting complications...

When you pay an amount, that amount will be either:

▶ an expense, such as electricity

▶ expenditure on an asset; that is, something of enduring benefit to the business such as a computer system or motor vehicle, or

▶ trading stock.

Expense classification

The first and major question to be asked is, 'Is the expenditure an expense or an asset?' Expenses, such as electricity, are treated as expenses for tax purposes (subject to private use) and deducted from your income. The purchase of trading stock is also a deduction as part of your cost of goods sold. Expenses as such are treated the same under the GST and income rules—that is, they are accounted for when the obligation is created (accrual) or when payment is made (cash).

Depreciating assets

Micro businesses can treat expenditure of up to $1000, irrespective of the fact that the outlay is in fact in relation to what would normally be a depreciating asset.

For other small businesses that limit is $100. Quite a noticeable difference.

If the outlay is over the limit and is in relation to an asset of the business, then the rules change again. Assets are subject to GST when the obligation is created (accrual) or when payment is made (cash) in the same manner as an expense.

However, for income tax purposes, assets are subject to a depreciation charge (*decline in value*, in tax terminology) once they are installed and ready for use.

Other issues regarding expenses

As you are operating on a cash basis, you record your expenses only when you actually pay them. Even if you have the invoice at the end of the accounting year, you cannot take the expense into your books until you actually pay the account. Under the accrual rules it is when the obligation is cast.

Exceptions to this rule, where expenses are treated the same, concern outstanding PAYG and superannuation on behalf of your employees. They are accounted for as they are paid, and provisions for your employees' annual leave are not a tax expense until they actually take the leave. Generally small businesses do not make such accounting provisions.

When to record a payment under cash accounting rules

To pay an account is to settle the account, and this can be by:

▶ cheque—the date of payment being the date of the cheque. Don't be tempted to 'kite' (that is, manipulate the cheque date—it is too easily picked up in a tax audit). The date of the cheque is assumed to be the date you posted it. If not, then use the date you posted it.

▶ credit card—the date of payment being the date on the credit card slip or, if paid over the internet, the date you made the payment

▶ direct debit to your bank account—the date the debit is entered into the account, not the date you receive the bank statement

▶ BPAY—the date of payment being the date you authorise your bank to make the payment.

GST issues

The final issue is the GST. If you are registered for the GST, the amount of the GST on the invoice (that relates to business use) must be separated from the expense and separately debited to a GST account. Only the 'net' amount—that is, the invoice price less the GST component—is debited to the expense or asset account. Of course, the whole amount is credited to the bank to balance out the double entry in your accounts.

And that brings us to another issue with the GST. You can claim the GST on expenses, called an *input tax credit*, only if you have a tax invoice from your supplier. No tax invoice—no claim! And you can only claim the amount of GST that is shown on the invoice. Some suppliers, such as council rates, do not have a GST component, and some businesses with income less than $75 000 are not registered for the GST and therefore do not claim it, so the golden rule is that all expenses must have a tax invoice and only the GST shown on the invoice can be claimed. Businesses not registered for the GST (such as the lawn mower man) can still give you a tax invoice; it is just that it will not have any amount of GST shown on it that you can claim.

The Tax Office will audit your GST claims at some stage. Make sure your filing system allows you to quickly find any tax invoice the GST auditors may require. It is normal practice for them to select a number of invoices at random and ask you to produce the originals on demand. Be ready!

If your supplier cannot give you a tax invoice that includes an ABN number, then you must withhold 49 per cent of the invoice amount and send that to the ATO with your next BAS. If your supplier cannot give you a tax invoice, find another supplier who can. No tax invoice—no business dealings!

Business expenses incurred by yourself as an individual for your business

The golden rule is you are not your 'business', which is a separate entity all on its own. Problems can arise when you purchase items for the business using your own personal account, such as a Visa card in your name. If you are an individual in business this is not a real problem, but if you are in partnership or a company then you could have a problem.

Make absolutely sure all such purchases are recorded in your business against your drawings account. Under no circumstances should you attempt to deduct such purchases from your own personal earnings on your own tax return.

Prepaid expenses

When you pay your annual insurance on your motor vehicle you are actually paying the account in advance. Examples of some other common prepaid expenses are professional association fees, software support fees, council rates, water rates, and even your telephone or PABX rental.

If you are a micro business with a turnover under $2 million and the payment is for less than $1000, or is in the nature of wages or salary, or is a payment by court order, then you can claim it as an outright expense. For other small businesses any other prepaid expense is not an allowable deduction until the service has been provided.

Under the small business concessions, as a micro business with a turnover under $2 million you can claim other prepaid expenses outright provided that you do not prepay more than 12 months in advance, and the period it covers ends no later than the end of the next financial year. However, in the unlikely event that the payments cover a period in excess of 12 months and are greater than $1000, you must apportion it over the financial years concerned.

Bank accounts

When you pay an invoice you credit the bank account and debit the expense account (and the GST account, if appropriate). For income amounts you debit the bank account and credit the income and GST account. But what about when a customer pays by credit card or we pay our accounts by credit card?

For income it is not a problem. Credit card slips or direct debits are debited to your bank account as if they were cash. However, when you make credit card payments they are taken into your books at the time of payment by the credit card, not at the time of payment of the credit card statement. If you are handling your credit card as a liability account, then you would enter the payment against that account. But what about the situation where subsequently you pay only the minimum amount off the credit card? In this instance you are effectively borrowing funds from the bank and the credit card account is now a liability, although in practice most credit card accounts are held with the bank accounts and are treated as you would an overdraft. Interest paid on the credit card, to the extent that the purchases were for business purposes, is a tax-deductible expense.

Accounting for loan repayments

Business loans that are formal loans with loan agreements and so on, as distinct from credit card loans, are usually either in the form of a bank overdraft or a business loan. The fees and interest you pay on these loans, to the extent that the loan monies have been used for business expenses as distinct from personal expenses, are expenses that can be offset against your income for tax purposes. The principal repayments do not affect your taxable income.

If you are using a bank overdraft facility, you account for the fees as part of the 'bank reconciliation' process. An overdraft account, usually a cheque account, is often treated just like any other bank account — that is, as an asset but with a negative rather than positive balance. When you draw funds out of a bank overdraft those funds are not income to the business; rather, they create a liability, albeit accounted for as a negative 'bank account' asset. It is the interest and fees on that overdraft that are transferred each month into an expense account.

For a business loan the accounting is a little more complex. When you receive the money, say $100 000 by cheque, you bank the cheque in your normal operating account and create a liability account to hold the outstanding balance.

    Dr   Bank account (asset)   100 000
      Cr   Loan account (liability)   100 000

When a repayment is made, the interest component is an expense and only the principal repayment comes off the liability account. If you make a repayment of $3000 and you know that $300 of this amount is interest, then:

    Dr   Loan account (liability)   2700
         Interest expense   300
      Cr   Bank account   3000

However, it is normally not practical to distinguish the components of each repayment, therefore the repayments are usually offset directly against the liability account:

Dr   Loan account (liability)   3000
    Cr   Bank account   3000

At the end of each quarter you must then determine the amount of principal repaid and what's left is interest, fees and so on. Let us assume that you received the loan on 1 July and made three $3000 monthly repayments. It is now 30 September and your loan account looks like this:

		Debit	Credit	Balance
1/7/05	Business loan received		100000	100000
30/7/05	July repayment	3000		97000
30/8/05	August repayment	3000		94000
30/9/05	September repayment	3000		91000

On 30 September you obtain a statement from the finance company and determine that the outstanding balance (after the 30 September payment) is $91900. Comparing this to the account balance, you can see that the fees and interest amount to $900 for the period. You now journal this amount into the expense account.

Dr   Interest Expense account   900
    Cr   Loan account (liability)   900

The Interest Expense account now contains the fees expense and the loan account will now reflects the correct balance:

		Debit	Credit	Balance
1/7/05	Business loan received		100000	100000
30/7/05	July repayment	3000		97000
30/8/05	August repayment	3000		94000
30/9/05	September repayment	3000		91000
30/9/05	Quarterly interest		900	91900

Leased and hire purchase assets (includes assets under loan agreement)

The term *lease* can have different outcomes depending on whether it is an operating or financial lease. An operating lease is what we would call rent. A financial lease is what we would call a purchase. If we rent premises by a lease this is an operating lease; if we buy a car by lease, where we will own it at the end of the period, this is a financial arrangement.

It is very important to distinguish between a rental lease and a financial arrangement for purchase because they are handled very differently. Under tax law, a short-term hire agreement relates only to hourly, daily, weekly or monthly rental. Longer periods, including monthly rollovers, would probably indicate a 'purchase'. Hire purchase arrangements are always treated as purchases.

Rental leases

With a rental (operating) lease each lease payment is an expense (deductible in full) and the GST (as indicated on the rent invoice) is creditable in full, subject to any private use of the asset. However, you do not get any GST credit when you first start to hold the asset, nor is any depreciation available. If you account for income tax and the GST on a cash basis then you can claim the GST credit, and the income tax expense, when you actually make the lease payment rather than when the payment was due.

Purchase by financial lease or hire purchase

The treatment of the purchase of assets by lease or hire purchase arrangements is an area of concern, as the thrust of income tax law is to treat such items as a purchase and associated loan, whereas for cash taxpayers the GST requirements will allow for the GST credit to be claimed only upon actual payment of the lease or HP progressive payments, whether it is a true hire or in reality a purchase and loan agreement. A very complex approach to a very simple issue.

With the purchase of an asset by a finance lease or hire purchase, it is considered for income tax purposes that the purchase of the asset and the lease or HP agreement are two separate steps—one is a purchase and the other financing. When you pay a lease or HP payment you can only claim the interest as a deduction; the principal amount is written off the outstanding loan. You can also claim the GST credit applying to the principal component or administration fee but not the interest charge.

In the long term the practical difference between the two is negligible. *But,* a warning: do not claim both the GST credit and depreciation on purchase *and* the GST credit and full lease/HP payment. This is a common double counting mistake.

Given that the long-term difference between accounting for a lease as a purchase and as a rental is negligible, and because of the additional work required to account for a purchase as a depreciable asset, most businesses treat all leases as if they were rentals. Only when you finally purchase the asset at the end of the lease is it accounted for as a purchase. The only problem with this approach is that it is incorrect at law and additional problems arise if you have a trade-in. In these instances you are almost certain to account for the lease as a purchase.

If you are really 'purchasing' the asset using a lease arrangement, it is usually easier (and 'more' legal) to account for the lease arrangement as an outright purchase. In order to allow you to continue to treat a lease as a 'rental agreement', most lease agreements will contain a clause to the effect that ownership in the asset will pass back to the lease company at the expiry of the lease. A separate agreement will give you a right to purchase the asset for a predetermined amount. This is a prime example of what tax accountants call 'form over substance'. The lease agreement by itself is for the rent of an asset for a predetermined period, an operating lease, but taken together the agreement is for the purchase of an asset — that is a financial lease.

HP arrangements are always accounted for as a purchase for income tax purposes but as a 'hire' arrangement for GST purposes, excluding the interest charge.

Novated leases

Novation effectively means that the obligations under the lease are assumed by the employer while the employee works for the employer. Thereafter, the lease obligations revert to the employee. It is common for the lease agreement to be a tripartite agreement between lessor, employee and employer. Providing the supply made by the lessor is taxable, the employer will incur a GST component in each lease novation payment. These payments are deductible as an expense and you are entitled to claim the GST credit. These leases are not purchase leases but are treated as rental agreements. FBT applies to these arrangements in regard to any private use of the asset by the employee.

Private use of business assets

If your expense is partly for private use, such as an electricity account for both home and office, then you apportion the expense between the business and the private use — that is, you allocate the payment between the expense account for the business part and the drawings account for the private part. The GST-paid account will only contain GST paid on the business portion.

Apportionment

The entry for the apportionment is quite simple: you split the expense between taxable and private use. The complexity is in the GST. You can claim the GST credit only on the business use portion. Let us assume an electricity account for $132 on which one-third is for business use, say a home office. If you pay the account from business funds, this means that $88 is for private use and is debited to the drawings account and $44 is for business use and is debited to the electricity account. However, if you are registered for the GST, the GST component of the expense (1/11th) is debited against the GST paid account:

Dr	Drawings account	88.00	
Dr	Electricity account	40.00	
Dr	GST paid account	4.00	
	Cr Bank account		132.00

Because of the need to track expenses (say, motor vehicle expenses), you should keep all the same type of expenses together but at the same time account for each vehicle's expenses separately. For example, the 4321 code could be created for all motor vehicle expenses and than 4321.6 could be for petrol and maintenance, while 4321.61 is for the sedan and 4321.62 is for the delivery truck. All salary expenses, including superannuation payments and tax withheld from salaries, should be within the same group.

The main problem is with depreciating assets. If they are 100 per cent private use, then you treat them as above. If they are part business and part private, then you again use an apportionment approach. On purchase you only claim the GST credit on the business portion of the expense and you only claim depreciation on the business portion of the asset. This will be covered in more depth in chapter 4.

A note on fringe benefits tax

Fringe benefits tax applies to the private use 'employees' make of company assets. 'Employees' include company directors and their 'associates', which include family members. If your business structure is a company or trust, then FBT applies to any private use you, as the owners of your business, make of your company's assets, including using its cash for private purchases. Individuals in business as sole traders and individuals in partnership are not 'employees' of their business and therefore are not subject to FBT.

The private use of business assets by 'real' employees — that is, employees subject to the PAYG provisions — is subject to FBT irrespective of the business structure.

Your FBT obligations will be covered in detail in chapter 7.

CHAPTER 4
Capital allowances (depreciating assets)

Key areas we will cover in this chapter

▶ Capital allowances

▶ Low-cost assets

▶ Low-value pools

▶ When can I start to claim?

▶ How do I claim?

▶ Disposals

▶ Capital works

▶ Nominated assets

▶ Rental stock

▶ Primary producers

▶ Project pools

Defined terms we will introduce

Asset: an item you purchase that is of future benefit to the business

Depreciation: the process of writing off the purchase price of an asset over time

Capital allowance: the tax term for the depreciation provisions

Low-cost assets: assets with a total cost of less than $1000

Low-value assets: assets with an adjustable value of less than $1000

FOB *(free on board)*: the total cost of imported goods up to the port-of-departure, on which any customs duty is levied. For local purchases this refers to where you pick-up the goods from the point-of-sale

CIF *(cost insurance and freight)*: the total cost of imported goods up to the port-of-entry, on which GST is calculated. It is the FOB plus overseas freight, insurance and any customs duty. For local purchases CIF has the same meaning as FIS and is sometimes called the *Landed Cost*

FIS *(free into store)*: the cost price of any asset or stock item you purchase. It is the sum of all costs of any goods you acquire up your warehouse door (back dock).

The differences between tax terms and accounting terms are listed in table 4.1.

Table 4.1: tax terms compared with accounting terms

Tax term	Accounting term
Adjustable value	Written-down value
Balancing adjustment amount	Profit or loss on disposal
Balancing adjustment event	Disposal of the asset
Decline in value	Depreciation
Depreciating asset	Asset
Effective life	Effective life
First element cost	Cost of acquisition
Second element cost	After-market costs
Holder	Owner
Start time	Installed ready for use
Taxable purpose	Business use
Termination value	Proceeds of disposal

Under accounting rules, when you purchase an asset, you cannot claim the amount paid as an expense; rather, it is apportioned over the life of the asset and a portion of the cost is claimed as an expense each year. This process of apportioning and 'writing off' the purchase price as an expense is called *depreciation*.

The tax rules, called *capital allowances*, are very similar to accounting practice but with a few differences that we will explain as we go along. Unfortunately, to make thing even more complex there are two sets of tax rules in regard to asset purchases, one for small businesses and another for micro businesses with a turnover under $2 million. These are referred to as the *small business taxation concessions*.

In this chapter we discuss depreciation as an accounting concept as well as the tax concept of capital allowances and the small business tax concessions. The first question we must address is, what is an asset?

What is an asset?

When we spend money on a 'thing', to use the tax term, the first question we must ask ourselves is, what is the classification of the 'thing' that we are getting for our outlay? Accounts are classified for both accounting and tax purposes into six main categories:

▶ *Assets*—sub-classified into current, non-current and intangible

▶ *Liabilities*—sub-classified into current, non-current and intangible

▶ *Equity*—sub-classifications of equity depend on the business structure

▶ *Income*—sub-classified into income from trading and other income

▶ *Cost of sales*—cost of goods sold

▶ *Expenses*—sub-classified according to the business that you are in.

If we spend money it could be on an asset, to reduce a liability, to reimburse the owners, to refund our customers, to purchase trading stock or to satisfy an expense. The main problem that we will face is the question of whether our expenditure was on an asset or an expense; the others are usually more straightforward and clean-cut.

An expense (*revenue expenditure*, in tax terminology) is something of value that we have consumed or will consume within one accounting period of 12 months. Expenses are such items as electricity, rates, wages and motor vehicle expenses. They can be paid in advance but that does not alter their nature as an expense, only the timing of the deduction. We have already discussed prepaid expenses.

An asset (*capital expenditure*, in tax terminology), on the other hand, is something of enduring benefit to the company, something that will last and be of benefit to the business for more than 12 months—that is, more than one accounting period. Examples of assets are furniture, computers, plant and equipment, and motor vehicles. Some assets do not have a physical form, such as trade marks or patents, and these we call intangible assets. However, the value of the outlay has no relevance to whether or not the thing acquired is an asset. The only determining feature is whether it is of an enduring benefit that will last at least 12 months. A $20 fountain pen will correctly qualify as an asset under this definition.

De minimis non curat lex — the law does not concern itself with trifles!

Asset purchases are not only recorded in the general ledger but also recorded and tracked in an assets register. The de minimis rule is accounting jargon that means we should not record an expenditure as an asset where the cost of doing so outweighs the benefit gained from tracking that asset. In accounting we handle low-cost assets as an expense. The only question is what cut-off value we place on the outlay: are all outlays below $1000 to be treated as an expense?

When the new legislation that dealt with capital allowances was written, a de minimis rule was not included. However, under Law Administration Practice Statement PSLA 2003/8 amounts less than $100 (including the GST component) can now be treated as an expense, and all other capital items that cost less than $1000 (GST exclusive) are to be added to a low-value 'pool' and a deduction allowed at the rate of 18.75 per cent for the first year and 37.5 per cent for subsequent years, based on the reducing value method.

In a practical sense, if the total outlay is less than $100 then you classify it as a low-cost item in your expenses and write it off as an expense to that item. If it costs less than $1000 (that is, the business portion as discussed previously, and exclusive of GST), then you create an assets account called a low-value pool and allocate that expenditure to that pool. You do not record these low-cost asset purchases in your assets register.

All other asset purchases must be recorded both in your assets register and separately in your accounts under the appropriate heading, such as motor vehicles or plant and equipment.

Small business concessions

If you are a micro business able to access the small business concessions — that is, a business with a turnover under $2 million — then the rules that apply to your capital expenditure are different again.

A low-cost asset under the small business concessions (which can be expensed immediately on purchase) is:

▶ prior to the 2013 tax year $1000

▶ for the 2013 tax year and up until 31 December 2013 $6500

▶ from 1 January 2014 $1000

Compared to the $100 for other small businesses this is a major concession.

What is a depreciating asset?

Not all asset purchases are subject to depreciation. A depreciating asset is one that has a limited effective life and can be reasonably expected to decline in value over time. The prime exclusion to this is therefore land. Land is eternal and if anything appreciates over time and is therefore not considered to be a depreciating asset. Under law anything attached to land becomes part of the land and therefore items such as buildings, wells, dams and other earthworks are by definition not depreciable assets. Land and things attached to land have their own depreciation regime, which we will discuss later.

The next major exclusion is intangible assets such as trademarks, patents and goodwill. These are created by law and have no physical presence, and therefore again are excluded from the general term *depreciating asset*. Again, we will discuss these items separately at a later stage.

Our final exclusion will be motor vehicles. Motor vehicles are depreciating assets in their own right, but are also a very important expenditure for small businesses and therefore will be handled later in their own chapter. However, if you wish the business to claim all of the expenses of running the vehicle, or the business portion of running the vehicle, then you will depreciate the vehicle in exactly the same manner as any other business asset. (Note that the $5000 immediate write-off for cars introduced on 1 July 2012 ended on 1 January 2014.)

The following discussion will concentrate on the business portion of amounts expended on capital assets that are used in your business to produce assessable income.

Depreciating business assets

When you buy a business asset such as a computer, you first establish its business portion and include that business portion of the amount, net of the GST, in your assets accounts. The GST is also divided between the credit claimable (creditable acquisition) and a GST private use expense according to your estimated private use percentage.

Each year you can claim the business portion of the annual depreciation expense as a deduction. The private portion is a non-taxable expense. The depreciation expense is based on the effective life of your asset; or for micro businesses it is 30 per cent of the cost less accumulated depreciation (15 per cent in the first year).

When you sell or dispose of the asset, you divide any proceeds received into a business portion and the private portion amount based on your original business use percentage. You then calculate the asset adjustable value (written-down value), being the asset's cost less accumulated depreciation. The difference between the business portion of the sale price (net of GST—it is a taxable supply) and the asset adjustable value is either an allowable deduction or assessable income depending on whether or not the business portion of the sale price exceeds the adjustable value of the asset. Pooled assets and assets disposed of by micro businesses are handled slightly differently, as we will discuss late.

What is the cost of a depreciating asset?

There are a number of things we have to consider when we talk about the cost of an asset. In 90 per cent of cases, the cost of an asset is the invoice price, and that's that. But there can be circumstances where this is not the whole story.

An asset for tax purposes must be the complete asset. If you buy a computer system in modules, they were purchased separately.

The cost includes all expenses up to the point where it is installed and ready for use. Let us assume that you purchase an industrial lathe that must be installed and commissioned before handover. All costs of installing, including the footings, electricity supply and commissioning costs, will be accumulated into the one amount that forms the asset's cost base.

All after-purchase costs are also included; these are called second element costs. Let us assume that you purchase a second-hand truck and that you have the motor reconditioned prior to use; then that reconditioning will form part of the cost base of the asset. Similarly if you later add a towbar or sound system, these are second element costs included in the cost of the asset.

If you purchase an asset from overseas then all costs up to the point that it is handed over, installed and ready for use are included. These include the invoice cost of the overseas supplier up to the port of dispatch (the FOB price), the cost of overseas freight and insurance (the CIF price), any customs tariff paid, and all local handling and delivery expenses, but not the GST paid as part of the import clearance charges. Should there be any foreign exchange variations incurred in the purchase, they are offset against the cost of the asset to arrive at its cost for customs (the FOB money price paid) and for tax purposes.

How do I record the purchase?

Under normal circumstances you record the asset against its own asset account. Let us say we purchase a computer system for $2200:

```
Dr   Administration PC              2000
Dr   GST                            200
    Cr   Bank                                2200
```

However, if we decide that the business use proportion is 75 per cent (that is, the system is going to be used 25 per cent for private purposes), then the entry would be:

```
Dr   Administration PC              1500
Dr   GST                            150
Dr   Private use suspense           550
    Cr   Bank                                2200
```

The private use suspense account would normally be an equity account called simply 'drawings', irrespective of the business structure, and would be cleared at the end of the year.

An alternative to the above is to use an assets register to hold the details of all the business assets and just record the totals in the accounts of the business under such headings as Plant and Equipment. Both approaches are equally valid. However, in either case the business portion estimate must be recorded and will remain constant throughout the asset's life.

In some cases (for example, a machine that needs to be delivered and installed), the true cost will not be known until all invoices have been processed. That will entail a number of entries until the asset's value has been established.

When can I start to claim depreciation?

We have mentioned previously the idea of 'installed ready for use'. This is both a tax and an accounting concept. You cannot start to depreciate an asset until it is available for your use. It is important to record this date in your assets register, as it is the date on which all costs cease to be recorded against the asset (capitalised) and may start to be recorded as revenue expenses.

How do I calculate the depreciation to be deducted?

By definition an asset will reduce in value over time. It has an effective life. The term *effective* is not defined but is taken to mean that at some point in the future the asset will either wear out or become obsolete to the extent that it is no longer a viable business asset. Computer systems are usually obsolete well before they technically wear out, whereas trucks in the salt mining industry wear out very quickly.

You must determine the effective life in years and parts of a year for every asset you own. If you are a micro business using the small business concessions, then you may use five years for each asset irrespective of its true life. For other small businesses the Tax Office has produced the Effective Life Schedule (refer to an example of the schedule in Appendix A), which will list the effective life that the Commissioner of Taxation will accept without question for a wide range of asserts.

Two methods are used to work out the percentage from the effective life. The first is the *diminishing value method*, and this should be used in all cases where the alternative, the *prime cost method*, is not mandated by law.

Let us assume that you have looked up the tax ruling and found that the effective life of your asset is five years. The formula you use to convert this to a percentage is, firstly, 200% ÷ effective life—that is, 200 ÷ 5 = 40%.

The 200 per cent is referred to as an uplift factor and has been in effect since 10 May 2006, prior to which it was 150 per cent. The amount you can claim in the first year is prorated based on the number of days the asset has been in use.

As an example, let us assume we purchase a computer system for $3300 on 21 April. The amount is GST inclusive and we will be using the system 100 per cent for business purposes. How much can we claim in this year's tax?

Between 21 April and 30 June there are 70 days; use this over 365 to calculate the amount you can claim for depreciation this year:

$$3000 \times 70/365 \times 40\% = \$230$$

Next year you start off with the $3000 less what is already claimed at the full 40 per cent:

$$3000 - 230 \times 40\% = \$1108$$

Table 4.2 sets out how this is determined over time given:

▶ Date of purchase: 21 April 2014

▶ Effective life: 5 years

▶ Purchase price: $3000

▶ Depreciation: 40 per cent.

Table 4.2: calculating depreciation on a computer

Year	Written-down value	Depreciation allowed
1	3000	230
2	2770	1108
3	1662	665
4	997	399
5	598	239
6	359	144

Of course, the depreciation in the above case is handled in your books in exactly the same way as you would in the accounting world. Each depreciable asset has one chart of account entry that holds the asset (Dr Balance) and immediately following this is an accumulated depreciation account (Cr Balance) that holds all of the depreciation amounts that have been charged against the asset. In addition, you will have the one depreciation expense account that holds the depreciation expense for the year.

Dr   Depreciation expense   230
   Cr   Admin computer accumulated depreciation   230

You will notice from this that the written-down value (*adjustable value*, in tax terms) is below $1000 in year 4. In this year we will write the asset off the books by closing the written-down value to the low-value pool and depreciating the balance of that pool by 37.5 per cent.

Dr   Low-value pool asset   997
Dr   Admin computer accumulated depreciation   2003
   Cr   Admin computer   3000

This is the same pool we use for assets purchased under $1000.

Small business concessions for businesses with an annual turnover under $2 million

Technically all micro business assets above the concession amount ($1000 or $6500, depending on the year of purchase) are recorded in the one pool, which is depreciated at the rate of 30 per cent. However, this treatment would be inconsistent with good accounting practice. It is far better to handle the asset purchases as you would in a small business but with a 30 per cent rate being used and 15 per cent in the first year, irrespective of the date of purchase.

Similarly any assets with a balance of less than $1000 are written off the books and the balance placed in a small business pool and the pool balance continues to be depreciated at the rate of 30 per cent. It should be noted, however, that if the balance of all your small business assets, including the pool balance, should fall below the concessional write-off amount (currently $1000), then you can write off all of your assets balances as a depreciation 'low-value' expense in that year.

Disposal of a depreciating asset

This is where a micro business differs from the normal small business. Firstly, disposals in the normal course of business: these can occur through sale, trade-in (which is treated as a sale and purchase separately) or scrap. Any expense that we incur in selling or disposal of the asset, decommissioning costs and so on are included as a second element cost of the asset.

You can now proceed in one of two ways: the traditional method is to create an account called Disposal of Assets and write the asset's value and accumulated depreciation value to that account. Alternatively you can just use the asset account itself and write the accumulated depreciation off to that account. This is the easiest option in computerised accounting.

The next step is to write off the proceeds of the disposal, called the *termination value*, to the account you choose to use. But there is a complication here:

▶ If you claimed the GST credit on purchase, then 1/11th of the business portion of the disposal value is considered to be a GST adjustment and is written back to the GST account.

▶ If the business percentage is less than 100 per cent, the disposal value is to be divided between the business value of the asset, to be credited to the asset account and the GST account, and the private portion of the account, to be credited in full to your drawings account.

The asset account, which is normally a debit balance account, will now hold:

▶ the original debit entry of the cost of acquisition

▶ plus any additional costs incurred, called *second element costs* in tax terms, less

▶ the full amount of any depreciation expense that you have claimed against the asset, the balance of its accumulated depreciation account, less

▶ any proceeds of sale or disposal, called its *termination value*, net of GST.

The balance of the asset account can either be a debit value that represents an amount to be expensed and treated as an allowable deduction or a credit amount that is to be included in your business income. For accounting purposes they are treated as Other Income/Expense amounts, but the Tax Act makes no such distinction and refers to the amounts as a balancing charge event, with an amount to be included in either your assessable income or treated as an allowable deduction as the case may be.

If the disposal value is in excess of the original cost, then you have a potential capital gain. If the asset has not been used 100 per cent as a business asset, then the private portion would be subject to a capital gain, then it is treated as any other private capital gain, except for micro business where private capital gains on the disposal of business assets can be ignored.

You should note that for accounting purposes it is very important that you correctly classify the profit or loss on disposal of an asset as either an Other Income or Other Expense item, as appropriate. This is to ensure that the amounts do not become entangled in your budget reports, which entails a comparison of your actual trading income and expenses compared with your predicted amounts without any extraordinary amounts included. Cash flow, of course, is another matter entirely.

Pooled assets

There are two types of pools:

▶ If you are a small business, then you will have a low-cost pool that holds all assets purchased with a value of less than $1000 and all assets that have been written off to the pool because their written-down value (adjustable value) was less than $1000.

▶ If you are a micro business able to access the small business concessions, then the sum total of all your depreciable assets is considered to be in a small business pool.

If you dispose of an asset held in a low-cost pool, then you add to that pool any additional costs incurred in the disposal of the asset, their second element costs, and then credit the pool with the business portion of the disposal proceeds net of the GST adjustment. If as a result of these actions the total value of the pool is still in debit, then you continue to depreciate the pool at 37.5 per cent per annum in the normal way. However, if the balance at the end of the financial year is in credit, that amount must be immediately written off as an Other Income amount and included in your assessable income.

Disposal of pooled assets — small business concessions

For micro businesses the process is identical to this, with the small business pool being used, with the exception of three circumstances:

▶ If, as suggested, you keep your main assets separate from the pool for accounting purposes and only roll them into the pool once the written-down value falls below $1000, then the treatment is slightly different. Any balance amount left over is not accounted for as an Other Income/Expense amount but rather is added to the small business pool.

▶ If the small business pool balance is in credit, provided that the total of all of the depreciation amounts of all your depreciable asset, including the pool, is still in debit, then you can continue to depreciate the pool in the normal manner, albeit as a credit adjustment to the depreciation expense rather than a debit addition.

▶ And if after disposal of the asset the total of all the written-down values (adjustable values) of all of your assets including the pool is in credit, all of your assets must be written off to the pool and the credit balance treated as other income/assessable income.

Involuntary disposals

If you disposed of an asset against your will, as in the case of a fire, and you receive a compensation payment, that payment would be treated as a termination value and you could be liable, in normal circumstances, to a balancing charge event. However, if the disposal was involuntary, then any accounting profit you make on the disposal can be rolled over and deducted from the cost of the replacement asset, provided the replacement is made within 12 months.

Capital works

The business assets that we have been discussing would fall into the accounting meaning of plant and equipment but not land or anything attached to the land. *Capital works* is a term used to cover the construction types outlined in table 4.3 (overleaf).

Table 4.3: capital works deductions

Construction type	Tax rate
Construction of short-term travellers' accommodation including hotels, motels, guesthouses or apartments, all of which must have at least 10 rooms to qualify	From 1982: 2.5 or 4 per cent Currently: 2.5 per cent
Construction of non-residential buildings used for industrial activities, such as manufacturing operations, processing primary produce and cold storage of perishable goods, but not the preparation of food or drink in retail outlets	From 1979: 2.5 or 4 per cent Currently: 4 per cent
Construction of non-residential buildings used for research and development	From 1985: 2.5 or 4 per cent Currently: 2.5 per cent
Construction of non-residential buildings used for other income-producing activities	Since 1992: 4 per cent
Structural Improvements, such as sealed roads, driveways and car parks, bridges, pipelines and associated earthworks.	Since 1992: 2.5 per cent

The allowable deduction for capital works is based on the initial construction cost. The percentages that apply are fixed at the time of construction, as is the cost base. The deduction is based on a flat percentage of that construction cost.

If the item is sold then the new owner is entitled to an allowable deduction for any remaining deductible amount, based on the percentage that was in place at the time of construction and on the original construction cost, not the purchase price. The new owner will require a certificate from the seller outlining the construction cost, the percentage applicable and the amount of the original construction cost that is still available.

There is no balancing charge event in relation to capital works, but any subsequent capital gain or loss from disposal of the building is adjusted for any amounts claimed as a deduction.

Nominated assets

There are some assets that have been specifically mentioned in the Tax Act and you can (and must) use these nominated rates, whether or not they fall within some other general item. This is just one example of the more general tax law that the specific takes precedence over the general.

Software

Off-the-shelf software, called in-house software for tax purposes, purchased either in a box or over the internet, is a business asset and is treated as such. Boxed software is depreciated at a fixed rate of 25 per cent over four years, the first year being pro-rata over the days held.

Where software is being developed for your business, you create a software development pool and allocate all of the costs of development to that pool. A separate software development pool is created for each year and the pool balance is written off at a rate of nil for the first year, 40 per cent for years 2 and 3 and the remainder in year 4.

Intangible assets

Intangible assets are rights created by law; they are by nature intangible in that they have no physical form. Such assets are depreciated by the prime cost method over their statutory effective life; that is, by their life as set out in the Tax Act. Examples of the main intangible assets covered are listed in table 4.4.

Table 4.4: examples of tangible assets and their effective life

Intangible asset	Effective life
Standard patent	20 years
Innovation patent	8 years
Petty patent	6 years
Registered design	15 years
Copyright (except in a film)	25 years (or, if less, until copyright ends)

For example, we register a design that has cost us $30 000 to develop and to register. We can now depreciate that design by $2000 per year for 15 years.

Blackhole expenditure

Some business expenditure is capital in nature but not specifically covered in the Tax Act. This is usually referred to as *blackhole expenditure*.

This expenditure can be an allowable deduction at the rate of 20 per cent per year over five years and covers such items as:

► expenditure incurred to establish your business structure

► expenditure incurred to convert your business structure to a different structure

► expenditure to raise equity for your business

► expenditure to defend your business against takeover

► costs incurred in an unsuccessful takeover attempt

► costs incurred to stop carrying on your business such as liquidation and deregistration costs.

Depreciating 'rental' stock

Purchases of inventories for resale are expensed on purchase to either the purchases account or inventories, depending on the method of inventory accounting being used. However, goods that you buy to use in a rental business are not considered by the tax laws to be trading stock; rather, they are assets. As an example, let us assume you run a fancy dress shop. Your 'stock' in this instance is not trading stock, but rather assets that you have purchased as part of your rental stock.

This is one example where a micro business can use the 'small business pool' with effect. In a business such as a fancy dress hire shop or party hire business, a number of items will always go missing; you may charge for these or you may not. Are these sales or disposal of an asset? How do we handle the complexities of such businesses?

The answer from a general accounting perspective is quite simple. You put all of your rental goods into an asset pool. You then amortise this pool of assets at 30 per cent per year on the opening balance. Any items added to the stock during the year are amortised at 15 per cent. The value of any 'sales' or forfeited bonds are subtracted from the pool balance and are not included in your sales figures. Of course, all additions are net of the GST where appropriate. Table 4.5 and the calculation that follows illustrate the process.

Table 4.5: using the small business pool—an example

Opening stock 1 July Y1	$856 000
Purchase of stock during the year	120 000
Forfeiture of bond from non-return	15 345
Closing stock before depreciation charge	960 655
Depreciation expense	262 499
Opening value 1 July Y2	698 156

Depreciation calculation:

$$30\% \text{ opening value } \$856\,000 \times 30\% = 256\,800$$
$$15\% \text{ of additions } \$120\,000 - \$15\,345 = \underline{5\,699}$$
$$\text{Depreciation expense} \quad 262\,499$$

You could of course keep a separate 'asset pool' for each class of assets (say, formal wear, general costumes, novelty items) or just the one pool.

A small business that cannot access the small business concessions can still use the low-cost pool for this purpose where the items purchased for the rental business are below $1000 each. In all other instances the assets have to be accounted for individually. This would be the case in a machinery rental or motor vehicle rental business.

However, the above is accounting for the items only from a general ledger and taxation perspective. You would still need to keep separate inventory records to manage your stock levels.

Primary producers

Just because you have a couple of olive trees in the back yard does not make you a farmer. To be a primary producer you must enter into the business in a methodical manner with an expectation of profit. You must be able to prove this expectation, preferably by a business plan and projected budget. If you fail this test but still feel that you are in business, you should seek professional assistance in order to examine other alternatives available.

Primary production takes many forms, from wine-making and fruit-growing to animal husbandry (raising live stock for sale). Given that you are in fact 'in the business' of primary production there are a number of special provisions that will apply to you.

Most of your depreciating assets, such as your tractor, are handled in the same manner as other small business taxpayers. However, as illustrated in table 4.6, some items get special treatment:

Table 4.6: depreciating assets — some special cases

Water facilities	These refer to plant for conveying or conserving water (e.g. dam, tank, bore, irrigation channel, pipes; new not second-hand).
	You can deduct 1/3rd of any expenditure on buying or improving water facilities over three years including the year in which you spent the money.
Grapevines	25% per year, pro-rata in the first year
Horticulture plants	If their expected life is less than three years, then you can deduct any expenditure up front.
Land care	This may refer to eradicating pests and weeds, fencing (for pest control), drainage and salinity control. You can deduct this expenditure when you incur it, excluding any expenditure on plant discussed above.
Electricity connection	10 per cent per year for each year over a 10-year period
Telephone lines	10 per cent per year for each year over a 10-year period

Stud or working animals would be considered assets and depreciated accordingly.

Project pools

This explanation of capital allowances is just a summary of the Tax Act position. It will be sufficient for about 90 per cent of small businesses, but for businesses in the business of project development there is another set of rules that deal specifically with projects. These are referred to as *project pools*. The basic concept is that you pool all your expenditure on a nominated project, such as a mine development, and then depreciate or amortise that project cost over the life of the project.

You should note that these rules are quite restrictive and apply only to very specific types of expenditure that are not deductible elsewhere. This includes mining capital expenditure, expenditure to create or upgrade community infrastructure, some site preparation costs for depreciable assets, feasibility studies, environmental assessments, information costs (such as mining exploration reports), intellectual property, and ornamental trees or shrubs.

A footnote on the $300 immediate write-off

As already mentioned, small businesses that are unable to access the small business concessions can only write off an asset that has a GST-inclusive cost of less than $100. Many small business owners believe the limit is $300. This is incorrect.

The $300 (net of GST) immediate deduction is only available to taxpayers who use the asset for the purpose of producing assessable income that is not income from carrying on a business—for example, an asset used in a rental property such as whitegoods costing less than $300.

CHAPTER 5
Trading stock (inventory)

Key areas we will cover in this chapter

▶ Trading stock

▶ Taxation of trading stock

▶ Valuation

▶ Annual stocktake

Defined terms we will introduce

Trading stock: an item that you purchase in the normal course of business and that you intend to resell at a profit

Consumables: items of small value you use in your business that are not separately identified on your customer's account

Periodic: accounting for inventory by 'periodically' calculating the cost of goods sold

Perpetual: accounting for inventory in such a way that the cost of goods sold of any item of inventory is immediately recognisable

Closing stock: the quantity and value of your trading stock at the end of the financial year

Opening stock: the carry-forward amount of your closing stock from the previous year

Trading stock, sometimes called *inventory*, is the goods you purchase in the normal course of your trading activities that you intend to resell at a profit. A simple example is the milk held by your local deli. They purchase milk at a wholesale cost and sell it to you at the higher retail price, making a 'margin', or profit, on the sale.

Another example is the tradie's van. Let us assume that the tradie is an electrician. In addition to the bundles of cables, clips and screws they carry, they will also carry electrical fittings, such as switches, light fittings and fans, that they will have purchased at 'trade' price. The stock of electrical fittings is their trading stock, to be itemised on a client's account at a retail price.

What about the cables, clips and screws? These items, in a small business sense, are usually referred to as consumables and would be expensed on purchase. The only questionable item would be the cables. If you charge your customer by the metre for cable used, then you must account for it as trading stock. If you simply include a standard amount in your quote as the overall cost of the job, then it is a consumable.

Most tradies — electricians, plumbers, mobile motor mechanics and dog washers — would account for their stock items as either consumables or trading stock depending on the cost and whether they invoice their customer as a separate item on the invoice.

When you purchase items that you are going to identify separately on your account, you will debit the purchase to a purchases account in a manual system or to an individual inventory account in MYOB. When you purchase miscellaneous items of low value that you are not going to account for as individual items, you simply debit that purchase to an expense account called Consumables. I discuss the account for trading stock in greater detail in my book *Learn Small Business Accounting in 7 Days*.

The value of your trading stock

When an electrician goes down to the local hardware store to buy a fan to be installed in a client's premises, there is not much doubt as to the cost of that item. It is the cash register price less the tradesman's discounts — the trade price.

However, not all purchases are that simple. Trading stock and assets share a common valuation base inasmuch as both are valued at your back door; that is to say, all costs up to the point that your trading stock has been delivered to your premises are included. In the case of overseas purchases, this includes any foreign exchange adjustments required. In the case of local purchases, all costs incurred in getting the goods from your supplier to your back door are included. This cost would take in local cartage and insurance.

In the case of an overseas purchase, your invoice price is usually stated at FOB—that is, all costs up to the point of export in the country of purchase. To this you have to add:

▶ overseas freight and insurance

▶ costs of local customs clearance

▶ inspection fees, if any

▶ customs duty

▶ local cartage and insurance

▶ any cost associated with foreign exchange movements.

It should be noted here, of course, that the purchase value of trading stock entered into your system is normally net of the GST amount. The GST component is treated separately in the GST account. The only exception to this rule is where you are not registered for the GST, in which case the purchase price recorded is the full amount inclusive of any GST component.

Timing?

However, the timing of just when you do record your purchase gets a little messy.

If you are a micro business—that is, you have a turnover under $2 million—then you can record your purchases when you actually pay for them. For example, if I purchase an item on my trade account I will record the item only when I settle the account at the end of the month. This is referred to as a cash accounting. If, however, your business has a turnover of more than $2 million, then you record the invoice details and the subsequent settlement of the account in two steps. This is normal business practice and is called accrual accounting.

Now it gets messy! What if I am an electrician and I purchase a fan on my 30-day trade account, as is normal practice, for a client and complete the installation that day? If I am a micro business electrician I do not record the fan purchase until I settle my trade account, so I cannot invoice the client until after the end of the month. Clearly this is not acceptable.

There are two alternatives. First, you could issue the client with a manual, handwritten invoice, collect payment on the spot and worry about the formal business accounting at a later date. This is normal business practice for a lot of tradies working as sole traders. The second approach is to use the 'cash accounting' option in your computerised accounting system, such as MYOB. Under this option you run your accounts according to normal accrual accounting practice—that is, you enter the invoice on purchase and then enter the payment on settlement. The difference between using this approach as a micro business and as a larger business is that you will 'report' under the cash accounting option whereas a normal business will just report under the normal accounting practice. This is covered in Heather Smith's book *Learn MYOB in 7 Days*. Heather states, 'In MYOB you can view a profit and loss report prepared on a cash basis by looking under Accounts and then under the subheading Small Business Entity'.

You should also note that under MYOB it is only when the actual payment is recorded that it is recognised in the MYOB BAS, provided that your MYOB system has been set up for cash accounting.

A note on consumables

Consumables are items of small value that you purchase for use in the business but that are not itemised on a client's account. They include the nuts, bolts and screws mentioned above, but they also include your office consumables, such as pen and paper, computer ink and toner cartridges.

Items you purchase that are not going to be itemised on a client's account are not included in your inventory system; rather, they are applied to an expense account called Consumables. Often, for budgetary considerations, office consumables are separated from job consumables, and this practice is considered preferable as it allows you to correctly cost your jobs.

Under the Tax Act, consumables would normally be considered to be trading stock; however, if the amount of consumables on hand does not vary significantly from one year to the next, then the above accounting methodology will produce the correct taxation outcome. If at the end of the year the carrying value of your consumable stores, in your work van and in the office cupboard, is not reasonably close to the opening value at the beginning of the year, then you may have a tax situation to address.

The taxation of trading stock

In order to understand the tax approach, you must first understand the manual accounting methodology on which it is based. A cost of goods sold account in a manually prepared profit and loss account would look like this:

Opening stock	10000
Plus purchases	50000
Goods available for sale	60000
Less closing stock	12000
Cost of goods sold	48000

From this you will see that the cost of goods sold during the year was $48000 even though $50000 worth of inventory was purchased. In other words, we purchased an addition $2000 worth of inventory that was still on hand at the end on the year.

Of this items outline, the opening and closing stock figures are balance sheet items that do not play a direct part in the tax calculations. The purchases amount is an expense and is therefore an allowable deduction; however, it is $2000 overstated. This is where the tax calculation comes in.

Under the Tax Act, where the opening stock figure is greater than the closing stock figure, the difference is an allowable deduction. However, where (as in the example above) the closing stock figure is greater than the opening stock figure, the difference is included in your assessable income. The end result will be an allowable deduction of $50000 for the purchases for the period and an assessable income amount of $2000, giving us the net result of $48000 representing the cost of goods sold for the period.

The problem with this approach is when we account for our purchases under the perpetual method, as used in MYOB and other computerised accounting packages.

Under the manual accounting approach, purchases of trading stock are debited to an expense account called Purchases. This is known as the *periodic method* of inventory control. Basically you must do the above manual calculation 'periodically' in order to determine your cost of goods sold.

Under the computerised approach, your stock purchases are debited directly to the inventory asset account, or more correctly to that particular item's inventory subsidiary account. When you sell an item of inventory, that item's cost is debited directly to the cost of sales account and therefore the cost of sales account represents a real-time value of the cost of goods sold. There is no purchases expense account and no requirement for the periodic cost of goods calculation or inventory adjustment figures. When these figures are produced by your computerised accounting program in its tax report, they are simply a recalculation of the data to suit the outmoded tax legislation approach.

The small business concessions

If you are a micro business—that is, the aggregate turnover of all your business ventures is less than $2 million—then you can use the cash accounting methodology to record your stock purchases and sales. This means you get a tax deduction only when you pay for your purchases, not when you buy them, and you record your sales as assessable income only when you get paid, not when you invoice your clients. Exactly the same situation applied to the BAS and your GST credits.

As discussed, using the cash approach to record your inventory purchases and sales can cause problems when you use computerised accounting. You can find yourself in the situation of not being able to produce an invoice because you can't as yet record your stock purchases. The answer to this is to use normal accounting procedures, called accrual accounting, for your day-to-day business recording and to use the cash reporting options for your BAS and the profit and loss account.

The second concession that is directly related to trading stock is the fact that you do not have to record your end-of-year stocktake figures for income tax purposes if the variance in stock levels from one year to the next is less than $5000. This does not mean you do not have to do an annual stocktake, but rather you do not need to adjust your Assessable

Income/Allowable Deductions for the opening and closing stock levels if your trading stock value is reasonably close to last year's figures.

Of course, the only way to determine accurately if the value variation is within the $5000 limit is to do an annual stocktake. However, under the tax rules you have to undertake a stocktake only if you estimate that your stock level is more than $5000 different from last year's. If they are within $5000 of each other you can use last year's figure. It's your choice!

The annual stocktake

The prime reason we do an annual stocktake is called the *impairment test*. What we are doing is reviewing all of our stock for existence, damage, obsolescence, need and value:

▶ *Existence:* We determine and account for any theft of our trading stock, and we uncover any 'picking' errors that have occurred and adjust our records accordingly. For example, we are over one blue item but under one pink item. The obvious answer is that we have invoiced out a blue item but delivered a pink item instead.

▶ *Damage:* If any of our stock has been damaged in storage, then we need to rectify this by either disposing of or fixing the item concerned.

▶ *Obsolescence:* Often our stock items will become out of date because of movements in technology. We need to identify obsolete stock and take measures to move them off the shelf, for example through half price sales.

▶ *Need:* Over time our requirements and the needs of clients will change. Does our stock holding still reflect those needs or do we need to adjust stock levels to better reflect this changed situation?

▶ *Value:* Is our stock still worth its carrying value?

Trading stock valuation

Having adjusted our physical stock level to match our stock count, we now have to value our trading stock for both accounting and taxation purposes. It is normal practice to carry your trading stock at its cost price, the value you entered into your system from your supplier's invoice. If you wish, however, you can value your stock for both taxation and accounting at either cost, market price or replacement. You can also apply these rules selectively, valuing some stock at cost and other items at replacement or market value. Why would you want to do this?

The purpose of stock revaluation is to make sure that your carrying value truly reflects its actual value. If a stock item is obsolete its market value may be zero, or heavily discounted from its cost. If the cost of an item has fallen you might wish to value it at replacement, as you would if the opposite were true and the cost had risen dramatically.

By selectively assessing and valuing each stock item you will end up with a stock quantity and valuation that truly reflects your trading stock position.

Tax planning

It is a legitimate tax planning opportunity to value your trading stock for tax purposes at something different from what you value your stock for business purposes. As an example, you are a micro business and after carefully reviewing all your stock you determine a total value of $5200, whereas at cost it is only $4800. You would therefore be within your rights to adjust the stock values in your records to what you consider are the correct values, but for tax purposes to remain with cost.

For larger businesses the tax adjustment rule can cause some problems where the closing stock figure is greater than the opening stock figure and the difference has to be included in your assessable income. It would make sense to value your closing stock using one of the options available to you that would minimise its value.

You should also be aware that:

▶ you can only adjust the closing stock figure, and once set this becomes the opening stock figure for next year, and therefore

▶ playing with trading stock valuations is only a timing issue. What you adjust for this year is just as likely to come back and cause you more problems next year.

Other issues

Over the years I have been asked many questions on this subject and I have raised a few of them here. If you have any queries of a similar general nature, please email me at rod@tpabusiness.com.au and I will answer them in the Q&A section on my website at www.tpabusiness.com.au.

Work in progress

But what about a partially complete home? Can the builder take this into account? What about progress payments?

Progress payments are assessable income. Under normal circumstances you would account for these payments when you issue the invoice. However, a micro business (cash-based) taxpayer would account for the income only when the invoice was settled.

Work in progress is also to be included in your closing trading stock; however, only the work that has not yet been billed is work in progress. For example, if you issued an account at 'plate height' (brickwork complete), then only that part of the building above plate height is included as work in progress. The remainder, up to plate height, is completed.

The value of work in progress includes all costs that you have included as expenses in your accounts — the value of all material and all wages, for example — but does not include any profit margin.

Disposals other than in the ordinary course of business

In the case of an ongoing business, such a disposal would be as a result of destruction, as in the case of a warehouse fire, or as a gift. In the case of an insurance claim, the disposal value of the trading stock is the value of the insurance payout. In the case of a voluntary disposal, as in a gift, the disposal value is considered to be the market value of the trading stock in question.

If the acquirer is a business, as in the disposal triggered by a business restructure, the new business must value the acquisition of the stock at the same dollar 'market' value as set by the business disposing of the stock.

If the disposal is of obsolete stock, the business must prove that the stock is truly obsolete in that it has no reasonable expectation that the stock can be sold on the open market. In this case the business can value the disposal at a reasonable price. If they continue to hold the stock they can also revalue the obsolete stock to that reasonable price. The onus is on the taxpayer to prove that the price in both instances is reasonable and that the stock is in fact obsolete.

GST — food retailers

For businesses that purchase and sell both GST-*free* and GST-payable goods, accounting for the GST can be a problem. Please refer to the section on food retailers in chapter 9.

Private use of inventory

It is normal practice for the owners of small businesses to take items from the shelf or to purchase goods through the business. Let us take the example of a TV purchased by an electrical retail business for $3300. On receipt into the business the journal entry would be:

Dr	Television	3000	
Dr	GST	300	
	Cr Cash at bank		3300

However, this TV never reached the business premises but was delivered directly to the owner's premises; therefore we need to adjust the records by reversing this purchase:

Dr	Drawings	3300	
	Cr Television		3000
	Cr GST		300

The above transaction could just as easily have been an item of trading stock. You will notice that we did not 'sell' it to ourselves; rather, we just reversed out the purchase to the owner's drawings account, being careful to fully adjust the GST. The drawings account balance will have to be accounted for at the end of the year as either owner's salary or profit. How this is done depends on the legal structure of your business.

In some cases the owner's use of the business inventory cannot easily be accounted for, and to overcome that problem the Tax Office has issued a ruling on what the owners of these particular kinds of businesses would normally take from inventory in any given year. The latest ruling TD2014/2 was issued on 19 March 2014 (see table 5.1).

Table 5.1: value of goods taken from stock for private use for 2014

Type of business	Amount for adult/child over 16 years ($)	Amount for child 4–16 years ($)
Bakery	1310	655
Butcher	780	390
Restaurant/café (licensed)	4400	1705
Restaurant/café (unlicensed)	3410	1705
Caterer	3690	1845
Delicatessen	3410	1705
Fruiterer/greengrocer	760	380
Takeaway food shop	3300	1650
Mixed business (includes milk bar, general store and convenience store)	4070	2035

Please refer to my book *Learn Small Business Accounting in 7 Days* for a comprehensive look at accounting for trading stock.

GST and second-hand goods

As far as income tax is concerned, second-hand goods, such as in an antique shop, are handled just like any other items of trading stock.

For GST purposes, however, it is another matter. If you are registered for the GST and you buy and sell second-hand goods, then special provisions relate to that inventory.

If you buy your second-hand goods from another GST-taxable entity, and they provide you with a tax invoice for the sale, then the goods are handled in the same way as any other taxable purchase.

However, if you buy your second-hand goods from a non-registered entity, such as a deceased estate, then you can claim 1/11th of the cost to you as a taxable credit on three conditions:

▶ You charge GST on the sale.

▶ If you sell the goods for less than you paid for them, you receive only 1/11th of the sale price (a $300 minimum limit rule applies here).

▶ You can claim the 'special' credit only when you sell the goods.

Primary production — livestock

Your livestock raised for sale is considered to be trading stock for accounting and tax purposes, and you account for your sales and purchases of livestock in the same way as you would any other item of trading stock. As a micro taxpayer, if the difference between the value of last year's stock and this year's is less than $5000 you can ignore trading stock for tax purposes.

The cost you use is the item's cost, market or replacement price, just as with any other item of trading stock. Similarly natural increases of stock during the year can be valued at cost, market or replacement. If you elect to use cost, that cost can be either the actual cost or a cost prescribed by regulations — cattle or deer are $20 per head, pigs $12, emus $8, goats and sheep $4, poultry 35c. The cost of a horse by regulation is the higher of $20 or the cost of the insemination service fee attributable to acquiring the horse.

CHAPTER 6
Capital gains tax (CGT)

Key areas we will cover in this chapter

▶ Exempt assets

▶ Working out a capital gain

▶ Capital losses

▶ CGT effect on tax structures

▶ Residents and non-residents

▶ CGT small business concessions

▶ Death and taxes

Defined terms we will introduce

Active asset: an asset used in the business to produce assessable income

Capital gain: the excess of the disposal proceeds over the cost

Capital loss: the excess of an assets cost over the proceeds of disposal

Capital proceeds: the amount you receive on disposal of an asset

When you purchase an asset you are gaining something of enduring benefit. Whether it is a physical asset, such as a computer, or an intangible asset, such as company shares, you now own something of value. We classify this as a 'capital' expenditure. When you sell an item of capital you are just converting it from one capital asset to another—from a computer into cash, for example. No income is involved in this transaction and hence the transaction is not caught by the general provisions of the income tax law.

97

Introducing the CGT

In the 1970s and early 1980s a lot of our entrepreneurs made their fortune buying and selling real estate that, because of its capital nature, was not subject to income tax. This caught the eye of our legislators, who decided to implement a tax on the profits made from selling capital assets. This could have been done in one of two ways, through a separate Act and tax rate, or by including the profit as part of your normal income and taxing it as just one income amount made up of income from *all* sources, including capital profits. Australia chose this second option and hence since 20 September 1985 the capital gains tax legislation has been part of our general income tax law. However, the legislation applies only to assets purchased after that date. Any pre–20 September 1985 (pre-CGT) assets remain exempt from taxation to this day.

Another problem is evident here, however. Since September 1985, when you buy an asset you may not sell it for many years and as the profit you make is the difference between what you bought it for and what you sell it for, you are comparing old dollars with new. Inflation would distort this and make the profit seem greater than is actually the case. Initially the legislation allowed you to adjust the cost of the asset to reflect today's value, a process called indexation, and include only the lower indexed profit in your income. However, this process was considered too cumbersome and was done away with for assets purchased after 21 September 1999. After that date individuals were able to claim a 50 per cent reduction on the profits included in their taxable income from a CGT 'event', but for other taxpayers the whole amount is now assessable.

The other problem faced by the legislators was what to include? For purely political reasons they had to exclude the family home, your prime and principal residence, provided you had owned it for more than 12 months, but what if I sell my watch at a profit—do I have to include that in my tax? To overcome this anomaly, the legislation has an exemption for 'personal use assets' up to a value of $10 000 for each asset. This would cover most things in your home but perhaps not your caravan. If you own a personal use asset valued at more than $10 000 and sell it at a profit, then you must include the profit (or 50 per cent thereof) in your income tax calculations. If you make a loss on such an item it is disregarded. Personal use assets include collectables such as your stamp collection, but in this case the value is limited to $500 per item. Any profit on the sale of an item that cost more than this limit must be included in your tax calculations, but again any losses are disregarded.

Holiday homes, rental properties and commercial premises are not your prime and principal residence (note the singular), nor are they considered to be personal use assets. Such assets face the full force of the CGT legislation.

The next problem was cars. If cars and motorcycles were included most of us would accumulate capital losses that could be used to erode the revenue gain from this legislation. For this reason motor vehicles that can carry a load of less than one tonne or fewer than nine passengers are also excluded from CGT.

If you make a loss on the sale of a capital asset, other than an excluded asset such as your home, a car or a personal use asset, then you can carry that loss forward to be used against any future capital gain you may incur, but it is not deductible against your normal income.

CGT in summary

If you sell any asset, whether a physical asset or a right such as a share, you must include any profit you make in your taxable income unless it is an excluded asset such as:

▶ your home, provided you have owned it for more than 12 months (and haven't rented it out for more than six years)

▶ any personal use asset that cost less than $10 000

▶ motor vehicles that can carry a load of less than one tonne or fewer than nine passengers.

CGT in a little more depth

The first thing I should say is that tax law in Australia is the most complex of any nation on earth. Our legislation is twice the size of the US equivalent and the CGT code is one of the worst sections to interpret. The problem is that our legislators just keep adding to it without taking anything away. When they change a section they leave the old one and often give you a choice of which way to go. This makes interpretation a nightmare.

In this book I am covering the situation that will apply in 95 per cent of cases. There are always multiple exceptions that rarely apply but just could pertain to you. For this reason you should consult your tax accountant in all but the most clear-cut circumstances. This text will give you a good basic understanding of the CGT and make discussion with your tax advisor more comprehensible and meaningful for you.

Exclusions

From this point onwards I will be discussing the CGT as it applies to small business rather than to individuals. The first thing that we must address is the exemptions to the CGT that apply to a business (summarised in table 6.1).

Table 6.1: exemptions to CGT for businesses

Trading stock	It may appear obvious but your sales of trading stock are not subject to CGT. Trading stock is an asset but all income from its disposal is treated as income to the business, not as a CGT event. It is profit realised in the normal course of business.
Depreciable assets	Again, these assets are excluded as all income from the disposal is included as income to the business under the capital allowances section of the Tax Act. Please refer to the section on capital allowances for a more detailed look at this issue.
Private use	Any profit you make on the disposal of the private use portion of a depreciable asset is included in your taxable income unless you are a micro business. The CGT on the private use of business assets where the business can access the small business concessions is exempt from CGT.
Rollovers	In some very limited cases you can roll over the CGT profit into the cost base of a replacement assert. Rollovers will be discussed a little later.
Compensation	Compensation or damages received for any wrong, injury or illness is exempt, although it can sometimes be income in its own right.
Marriage breakdown	Any CGT triggered as a direct result of a marriage breakdown is ignored.
Superannuation	Rights, annuities and allowances paid out of an insurance or superannuation policy are exempt from CGT but may be included as income in some circumstances.
Micro business	A special retirement concession applies; we will discuss this later.

Working out the capital gain

The capital gain you make on the sale of an asset is akin to a profit calculation; in simplistic terms it is the selling price less the cost of the asset. The selling price is referred to as the *capital proceeds* and the cost of the asset is referred to as its *cost base*.

What are the capital proceeds?

Capital proceeds are the amount you receive for the asset minus any GST credit on the supply. If you receive goods in lieu, then those goods are valued at their market value.

What is the cost base?

The cost base is a little more complex. It consists of five elements that must be added together to determine the full cost base (after which further adjustments may be required). These elements are:

1   the money paid and/or the market value of any property exchanged to purchase the asset

2   any incidental cost incurred to the extent that it has not already been claimed as an allowable deduction, such as:

–   professional fees (accountant, broker, surveyor, valuer and so on)

–   transfer costs including any stamp duties paid

–   advertising and marketing for both purchase and disposal

–   search and conveyancing

–   borrowing expenses such as loan application and mortgage discharge

3   the costs incurred in owning the asset (if purchased after 20 August 1991) and where no allowable deduction has been claimed:

–   interest on money borrowed to acquire or refinance the asset

–   costs of maintaining, repairing and insuring the asset

–   rates and land tax

4   capital expenditure incurred in relation to moving, installing or preserving the asset

5   capital expenditure in establishing, preserving or defending your title to the asset.

Capital gains

In order to establish the asset's cost base you must determine all of the above and then add them all together.

If you acquired the asset prior to 21 September 1999 you may wish to use the indexing option to revalue the cost base. All elements of the cost base (with the exception of cost of ownership no.3) are subject to indexation. To index the cost base, first use the Australian Bureau of Statistics website to determine the CPI index for the quarter that you purchased the asset and divide it into the CPI index for the September 1999 quarter (123.4). Apply this to the total of your cost elements 1, 2, 4 and 5 and then add element 3 to determine your index cost base. Not exactly the easiest process, which is why it was replaced with the 50 per cent discount method, but this method applies only to individuals, not companies, and you can opt to use only one or the other. For individuals in business as sole traders, partnerships or trusts, the 50 per cent discount method will give you the best result. In very limited circumstances companies may be able to use the indexation method.

Having now established your cost base (or index cost base as the case may be), you deduct this from your proceeds of disposal in order to arrive at the capital gain. From this total you can now deduct any capital losses that you may have carried forward to get a net amount. For companies you add this net capital gain to your income on which you pay tax at the company rate, and for individuals who have owned the asset for more than 12 months you add 50 per cent of this amount (net of your CGT discount) to your income and pay income tax on your gain at your marginal rate.

This taxation methodology reveals a big difference between Australian capital gains tax and the tax's use in other OECD countries. Most countries have a separate CGT rate, whereas in Australia you just add the gain (or 50 per cent of that gain if applicable) to your taxable income and pay tax in the normal manner on the total amount. In effect, everyone can be taxed differently on the same capital gain depending on their own individual tax position, ranging from zero to the top marginal rate plus Medicare levy.

Capital losses

There are cases where your proceeds of disposal of an asset will not cover the cost base of the asset. In these cases a capital gains tax loss *may* be incurred. In order to determine if you have a capital loss you must first work out your 'reduced' cost base without the addition of the cost of ownership element no.3 and excluding from the cost base. This covers:

▶ any amount of the cost that was allowed as a deduction

▶ any amount claimed as depreciation under the capital allowances provisions

▶ any recouped costs not included in your income

▶ any tax offsets

▶ plus special case amounts such as certain amounts in regard to shares distributed prior to your owning the shares and any proceeds of illegal activities.

If after you have reduced your cost base by the above amounts it is still in excess of your proceeds of disposal, then you have a capital loss that you can firstly apply to any other capital gain you have this year; then, if there is still an amount left, you can carry this forward to be deducted against any capital gain you may have in the future.

If, on the other hand, your reduced cost base is now below your proceeds of disposal, then you are now in a situation where you have neither a capital gain nor a capital loss from the disposal of your asset.

You should note, however, that capital losses can be used only to offset a capital gain and cannot be used as a tax deduction against your normal income.

Australian residents versus non-residents

If you are an Australian tax resident, you will pay capital gains tax on any capital gain you make irrespective of where the asset happens to be located. A Singapore citizen who happens also to be an Australian tax resident will have to pay CGT on a Singapore apartment that they sell at a profit, irrespective of the fact that they also have to pay tax on the same transaction in Singapore. The tax paid in Singapore will be credited to the taxpayer when working out their Australian tax position, but such matters are outside the scope of this text.

In you are a non-resident for Australian tax purposes, then you will pay CGT only on the disposal of assets that were at the time of their disposal taxable Australian property.

Tax structures and income streaming

The term *tax structure* refers to the legal basis under which your business operates; *income streaming* refers to how the taxable income of your business is taxed and in whose hands it is taxed. We introduced this idea in chapter 1, but here we further refine the discussion as it relates to CGT.

Sole traders

From a tax perspective there is absolutely no difference in the capital gains tax consequences between the assets you own as an individual and the assets you use in your business. The cost base may vary because of the GST credits you may have claimed on the business portion of some of your asserts and because of any capital allowances (depreciation) you may have claimed on your business assets, but the tax methodology is the same. You calculate the reduced cost base, compare this with the proceeds of sale and include any capital gain, less the 50 per cent discount if applicable, in your assessable income or carry forward any capital loss you may have incurred.

Partnerships

At law a partnership is just a collection of individuals and therefore any capital gains tax event that happens to a partnership asset is considered to happen to the partner as an individual. In the case of an individual partner their own capital gain or capital loss position in relation to the disposal of a partnership asset is determined by reference to the partnership agreement and their claims on the asset in question. As a result, each partner has a separate cost base and reduced cost base for the partner's interest in each CGT asset held by the partnership.

Family trusts

Family trusts are the most common form of trust used by small businesses. In the case of a family trust, any capital gain or loss made by the disposal of a business asset held by the trust is usually taxable in the hands of the beneficiaries, as with a partner in a partnership. In the case of a trust, however, this is known as *income streaming* and is covered by very specific legislation in the Tax Act.

The Act requires that the trust deed allows for income streaming and that the trustee makes a beneficiary 'specifically entitled' to a capital gain by means of a trustee resolution. If the trust deed is deficient in this, or the trustee does not correctly make this resolution, then the capital gains are simply lumped together with all other trust income and assessed proportionally to the beneficiaries. This may result in a less than satisfactory tax outcome for the beneficiaries.

Small business concessions

Up to now we have defined a micro business as a business entity with an aggregate turnover of less than $2 million. This still applies to the CGT small business concession—with the addition of another test. If your business has an aggregate turnover in excess of $2 million but has net assets (total assets less total liabilities including provisions) of less than $6 million, then you will be able to access the small business concessions. The net asset test, like the $2 million turnover test, is an aggregate test of all your business entities, including affiliate and connected entities.

The small business concessions themselves apply to a CGT event that happened to an 'active' business asset used by yourself or one of your affiliate and connected entities. An active asset is one that the entity owns and uses, or holds ready for use, in carrying on a business and includes intangible assets such as goodwill, but active assets by this definition do not include depreciating assets where the gain or loss from their disposal is handled under the capital allowances regime. In addition, assets whose main use is to derive interest, annuities, rent, royalties or foreign exchange gains are not considered to be active assets and neither are those that have been active assets by the definition above for less than 50 per cent of the time they have been owned by the entity in question.

Provided that your business meets either the $2 million turnover criterion or the $6 million net asset test and the CGT event occurred to an active asset as defined above, then there are four small business concessions available to you:

▶ the 15-year exemption

▶ the 50 per cent reduction

▶ the retirement concession

▶ the small business rollover.

The 15-year (retirement) exemption

If you are over 55 and wish to retire or are permanently incapacitated, then you can ignore any CGT gains or losses made on active business assets that you dispose of, provided that you have held the asset continuously for a period in excess of 15 years.

The above concession applies to individuals in either a sole proprietorship or partnership arrangement. If your business structure is a company or trust, then to access this concession in relation to your share of the proceeds of the disposal of the active asset, you must be an entity's 'significant individual'. A business's 'significant individual' is one who owns at least a 20 per cent right to the distribution of income of the entity and must have done so for at least the 15 years that the entity has owned the active asset.

If you apply this concession, then the other three concessions do not apply.

The 50 per cent reduction

If you are a small business by the extended definition already outlined and you make a capital gain on the disposal of an active business asset, then that capital gain can be reduced by a further 50 per cent after you have applied any carry-forward or current year capital losses and applied the 50 per cent discount (if applicable). As an example, you sell your business for $600 000, of which $90 000 is a capital gain. You also hold $10 000 in capital losses:

Capital gain	90 000
Less prior year losses	10 000
	80 000
Less 50% discount	40 000
	40 000
Less 50% small business reduction	20 000
Assessable capital gain	20 000

This gain can then be further reduced by the small business retirement exemption and/or the small business rollover concession.

Small business retirement exemption

If you are a small business by the extended definition outlined, you can choose to claim an exemption of up to $500 000 where the proceeds of the sale of a small business are used for retirement. If you are the owner of a small business and you are over 55 and intend to retire, then you can claim this exemption. If you are under 55 at the time you make the claim, you can still use the exemption provided that you contribute an equivalent amount into a complying superannuation fund.

Following on from this example, if you were over 55 or were prepared to put the $20 000 capital gain made in the example into a complying superannuation fund, then you could also ignore the gain made under the 50 per cent reduction rule.

Again, the above concession applies to individuals in either a sole proprietorship or partnership arrangement. If your business structure is a company or trust, then to access this concession in relation to your share of the proceeds of the disposal of the active asset, you must be an entity's 'significant individual'—that is, one who owns at least a 20 per cent right to the distribution of income of the entity.

Small business rollover

If you are a small business by the extended definition and you dispose of an active business asset that you intend to replace with an equivalent asset, then you can claim rollover relief and disregard the capital gain provided that the asset is replaced within the period of one year prior to and two years after the disposal.

The replacement asset must be valued at least equal to the capital gain and must become an active business asset within the nominated period. If this does not happen the capital gain is reinstated.

Death and taxes

If you die your beneficiaries can use the above concession in your stead when working out the taxation position of the estate, provided that the CGT event happened within two years of your death.

CHAPTER 7
Fringe benefits tax (FBT)

Key areas we will cover in this chapter

- ▶ Fringe benefits tax
- ▶ Employee benefits
- ▶ Private use by employees
- ▶ Private use by owners
- ▶ Avoiding FBT
- ▶ Accounting for FBT
- ▶ Reportable fringe benefits

Defined terms we will introduce

Fringe benefits: any non-cash remuneration

Type 1: a benefit that includes a GST credit

Type 2: a benefit that has no GST credit

Gross up: to multiply the value of the benefit by the FBT factor

Reportable fringe benefits: a total grossed-up amount of the benefits received by an employee included in their payment summary

Up until the early 1970s the concept of remunerating an employee other than through a cash payment was almost non-existent. By the early 1980s, however, many firms were offering salary packaging deals whereby the employer would provide a benefit to the employee rather than paying a full salary. As the existing legislation in regard to such benefits was easily circumvented, many employees were gaining an unfair tax advantage over their salaried counterparts and pressure was put on the government to regulate this practice.

The government of the day could have approached this problem in a number of ways but decided to introduce a completely separate Act that enforced a penalty rate of tax on such fringe benefits in order to curtail the practice. How successful this has been is open to debate, but at least now salaried employees and those receiving their remuneration in the form of benefits are on a more level playing field.

Introducing the FBT

The *Fringe Benefits Tax Assessment Act* commenced on the 1 July 1986. It imposes a penalty tax on an employer, at the equivalent to an individual's top marginal rate including Medicare levy, on any benefits provided to an employee in respect of their employment. The term 'employer' here includes the employer themselves plus any associate or third party. The term 'employee' likewise includes the employee and any associate such as a family member. 'In respect of employment' includes past, present and future employees. Sole traders and partners in a partnership cannot be employees but company directors, including directors of trustee companies, can be considered as employees.

The benefits caught by the FBT Act are all-encompassing, the most popular being the provision of a vehicle or the right to use a company vehicle for private purposes. Others include low-interest loans, employee housing, entertainment, club fees, recreation, school fees, travel, car parking and many more. However, there are a number of exclusions, including:

▶ the payment of wages or salary, including termination payments

▶ cash allowances (except living-away-from-home allowance)

▶ cash superannuation contributions.

The exclusions are based on the fact that these payments are caught by the Tax Act itself.

There are also a number of benefits that would normally be caught under the FBT Act but that have been exempted from the tax. These include:

▶ employee subscriptions to professional journals

▶ newspapers and periodicals used for work purposes

▶ corporate credit cards

▶ airport lounge benefits (such as Qantas Club)

▶ use of employer's property on the work premises (such as private phone calls and tearoom facilities)

▶ relocation expenses incurred in moving an employee for work purposes

▶ minor benefits infrequently provided that total less than $300 per year

▶ taxi travel between work and home, or taxi travel provided to sick or injured workers

▶ transport companies providing public transport to current employees.

In addition to these exemptions there is the 'one item rule' that covers any one of the following provided it is used primarily for work purposes:

▶ one portable electronic device per year (such as a mobile phone or a desktop computer)

▶ one item of protective clothing

▶ one briefcase

▶ one item of computer software

▶ one item being a tool of trade.

It should be noted that the 'one item rule' does not apply to similar items issued to an employee for their use exclusively for work purposes, only items with a private use component.

The in-house benefits rule applies to employees' use of goods and services that are normally sold in the business (bread taken home by employees of a bakery, for example). An annual amount of $500 is exempt to each employee and FBT applies to any excess.

There are many more exemptions, such as worksite medical facilities and remote area benefits, that would not normally apply to a small business. There are also some benefits that are discounted, such as a 50 per cent reduction in the provision of remote area housing.

The only exemption that applies specifically to small business is car parking provided to employees. If you are a micro business (under $2 million turnover) or a small business (with a total income for the year of less than $10 million), then you can provide on-site car parking for employees without incurring any FBT liability.

Private use by your employees

All employees' private use is handled under the fringe benefits tax rules *irrespective* of the business structure. The main contenders here are motor vehicles, union fees, laptop computers, mobile phones, protective clothing (overalls), home phones and superannuation. I have deliberately mixed these up because the first thing to understand is that not all expenses are treated the same:

▶ Superannuation is FBT exempt; there are no FBT tax implications of providing superannuation for your employees.

▶ If your employees would get a tax deduction if they paid for the item, then there is no FBT implication under the 'otherwise deductible' rule; union fees fall within this category.

▶ If you provide items for which there is no private use, as in the case of protective clothing, then there are no FBT implications.

In all other cases you must account for the private use.

Accounting for the employee's private use

This can be done in one of two ways. *Firstly,* we can provide the employee with an allowance that is included in their salary, for instance a home phone allowance. With this the employee pays for the business use of their home phone. The allowance can either be a fixed amount or take the form of a reimbursement of expenses. Either way the allowance is taxed in the same manner as any other component of the employee's salary. It is up to the employee to claim the business use as a deduction against the allowance income in their tax return, and to justify the expenditure. In many ways, from an employer's viewpoint this is the easiest method, but claiming the GST credits on business use of employee assets may be a problem.

If you pay a fixed allowance each period, the GST credits could be lost; however, this is usually an insignificant amount. If the amount of the GST credit is substantial, you should ask the employee to make a claim on you (a reimbursement) for their business expenses, including copies of the original tax invoices. You can then reimburse them through their salary and claim the GST credits accordingly. The easiest way to handle sales representative motor vehicles expenses, for example, is to pay a fixed allowance to cover the purchase cost (business percentage of loan repayments) of the vehicle and then ask the employee to claim petrol and other expenses by reimbursement.

Secondly, we can pay the telephone account and claim the amount as a tax deduction against the business. Then we can have the employee reimburse the business for the private portion of the phone account, either by direct payment (income to the business or offset against the expense) or by deducting the private use amount from the employee's *after-tax* salary. Note that business use of home phones can only apply to phone calls, and those calls must be justified as business-related by written evidence, such as the phone bill itself identifying the call as business or a diary record. The home phone line rental should never be classed as a business expense.

If you use this second method, you must write back the private use portion of the GST credit claimed on payment of the account when the private use payment is made. This is more complex than the reimbursement method and for that reason the first method is preferable.

If we provide the employee with a business asset that they also use for private purposes, such as a motor vehicle or a computer, then we must also account for the private use portion by either of the above methods. If we do not seek reimbursement (an employee contribution in FBT terms) of the private use portion of the expenses paid or assets used, then that amount will be subject to fringe benefits tax.

Fringe benefits tax — categories of 'private use'

The fringe benefits rules contain a number of categories of expenses (ignoring motor vehicles, which are discussed later in this chapter), each of which involves its own calculations to determine the private use proportion. The last category is *residual benefits*, into which everything else falls. The main benefits that affect a small business are:

▶ expense payments

▶ property

▶ car parking (this does not apply to 'on-site' parking for small business)

▶ meal entertainment.

Expense fringe benefits refer to the value of any expenses the employer pays on behalf of the employee (such as school fees or club membership) or for which the employer reimburses the employee, other than by means of a taxable allowance as part of the salary package.

Property fringe benefits are made when the employer buys an asset such as a computer for an employee and gives that computer to the employee (ownership passes to the employee) for their own personal use. This is distinct from the employer providing the employee with *access to*, or use of, a computer that is normally work related only. The value of the fringe benefits is the value of the property provided less any employee contribution. The employee can then claim a deduction against their income for the business use of the asset.

Car parking fringe benefit applies only to small businesses (under $10 million turnover) where it is provided at a commercial parking station. Incidental parking (less than $100 per year) is exempt, as is work-related parking (as when visiting clients).

Meal entertainment fringe benefit applies when you, or your employee, take a client out to a meal. Under income tax rules the provision of meals for clients is not an allowable deduction. However, if you wish to use the FBT provisions you can deduct 50 per cent of the meal value and then *that* 50 per cent is subject to FBT. *Note:* as an employer you can spend $50 on each employee under this category (for a Christmas lunch, say) without incurring a fringe benefit and being allowed a tax deduction for the expense.

Other forms of FBT include:

▶ low-interest loans—the 'benefit' is the difference between the statutory interest rate of 6.45 per cent (for the 2014 FBT year) and the actual interest paid by the employee

▶ debt waiver—the benefit is the value of the debt written off

▶ the provision of housing by the employer—the 'benefit' is the difference between what the employee pays and what would be the normal commercial rent; note, however, remote housing is exempt if a number of conditions are met

▶ living-away-from-home allowance (accommodation and food)—subject to FBT if it is greater than what would be reasonable in the circumstances

▶ board (the provision of accommodation and meals)—the meals component is subject to FBT if in excess of a statutory amount

▶ residual benefits—this covers everything else. If you give your employee any benefits whatsoever, other than wages and salaries, superannuation and allowances, all of which are caught under the PAYE provisions, then you have a potential FBT liability.

Private use by company owners

For purchases by owners for their own private use out of business funds, the simple rule is that such purchases are debited to the drawings account and repaid in the form of a salary conversion. You do not claim the GST credit on private use purchases.

Part business and part private is best handled by apportioning the GST and crediting the drawings account with the balance. An item costing $110, of which 70 per cent was business use, could be apportioned $70 to the expense account, $7 to GST credit and $33 to the owner's drawings account. This is the same method used for individuals and partnerships, but for companies the drawings account must subsequently be converted into salary.

The main problem is with depreciating assets. If they are 100 per cent private use, then you treat them as above. If they are part business and part private, then the strict tax treatment for companies and company trustees is to claim the GST credit in full, debit the asset to a depreciation account and claim the depreciation in full (no private portion deduction). You then must pay FBT on the market value of the private use proportion. However, the Tax Office cannot advise you on how to determine the market value of this use.

The alternative method of dealing with depreciable assets used partly for private use, and one that must be used by sole traders and partners in a partnership, is to use the apportionment approach. On purchase you claim the GST credit only on the business portion of the expense and you claim depreciation only on the business portion of the asset.

An alternative treatment is available to the directors of companies or trustee companies. In these cases the owners, as 'employees' of the business, may elect to pay for their private use through the fringe benefits tax rules—that is, to lodge an FBT return and pay tax on private use at the FBT rate, currently the equivalent to the individual top marginal rate plus Medicare levy if applicable.

However, in the case where owners could use FBT, it is suggested that you adopt the 'contributory' method rather than pay the FBT tax itself. Using this method, owners account for private use through the drawings account. The contributory method can also be used for employees' private use, although an allowance method is simpler from a business accounting perspective.

If you decide to pay FBT rather than use the contributory method, your private use is taxed as a 'tax inclusive' fringe benefit. In this case your expense is 100 per cent income tax deductible and your GST 100 per cent creditable. The 'private use' tax consequences are incorporated into the FBT calculations.

A recap: private use by business owners

Fringe benefits tax applies only to employees of the business. Neither a sole trader business nor a partnership business 'employs' its owners, and therefore no FBT applies to private use by owners in these circumstances. The 'business profit' is your individual taxable income. You should make sure that any private use is deducted from your drawings account and not against business income. In this way the business profit will contain your private use and be taxed accordingly.

A company is considered to be a taxable entity in its own right and pays tax at the company rate. It 'employs' the owners. FBT applies to any taxable use of business assets by the owners of the business, be they directors, shareholders or their associates (your children).

Private expenses by owners of companies should be reimbursed through the owners' drawings account (by conversion into salary). This account holds the owners' drawings from the business and is usually (read *must be*) converted into a salary before the end of the income year, preferably on a quarterly basis. You must *not* have any funds outstanding in the drawings account at year's end. The golden rule: do not 'borrow' from your company.

As an alternative, companies can choose to pay FBT at the top marginal rate. You would have to have a salary that taxes any addition at the top marginal rate before you would contemplate paying FBT rather than offsetting the private use component through your drawings account.

How to avoid the FBT liability

As an employer, the easiest way to avoid FBT is to:

▶ pay your employees a wage that does not include any private use of company assets, or

▶ pay your employees an allowance to cover the business use of private assets that they own (such as home telephone account), or

▶ only provide exempt benefits to your employees, or

▶ ensure that your employees (including company business owners) reimburse the firm for the benefits received and/or the 'taxable' private use of the business assets. This is known as the *contributory method* but an important rule is that the 'contribution' must be from private after-tax monies. It cannot be a pre-tax salary sacrifice amount.

Accounting for FBT

If, as an employer, you find yourself with an FBT liability, you will be required to lodge an annual FBT tax return. The FBT tax year runs from 1 April to 31 March and you are required to lodge the return by 28 April. You will also need to register for fringe benefits tax. You will do this at the time you apply for your ABN. You can also register at any time after this should you need to do so.

The first step is to distinguish between the benefits provided that are subject to the GST and those that are GST exempt. To do this you would normally create two additional expense codes to hold these amounts:

▶ FBT Type 1—GST paid

▶ FBT Type 2—no GST.

The accounting methodology is to allocate to FBT Type 1 the amount of the benefit that includes a GST credit (if you are registered for the GST), and to allocate to Type 2 the expenses that do not include a GST credit (or all expenditure if you are not registered for the GST). These accounts will also help you reconcile your FBT paid on the BAS and the FBT return.

When paying the FBT tax you would normally allocate this to an FBT expense account. You should note that both the benefit paid and the FBT tax paid on that benefit are tax deductions for income tax purposes.

The theory behind the calculation of the tax payable on an employee benefit is quite simple but will take a little explaining. Let us start with a normal $100 received in the pay packet of an employee. How much did it actually cost the employer?

Assuming that the employee is paying tax at the FBT rate, being the top individual rate plus Medicare levy, currently 47 per cent plus 2 per cent Medicare levy, making a total of 49 per cent (for the 2016 FBT year), then you would have had to 'pay' the employee $196.08. It works out like this:

The gross amount of the payment is	196.08	(1.9608)
Less tax at the rate of 49%	−96.08	
Cash amount included in employee pay	100.00	

This is known as a Type 2 fringe benefit and would cover such benefits as payment of:

▶ an employee's private health insurance or medical expenses

▶ an employee's dependants' education fees to a school, college or university

▶ an employee's residential rent, or

▶ an employee's mortgage.

It also covers benefits paid to an employee of a business that is not registered for the GST—that is, one that operates under the GST minimum limit.

If you, as the employer, were able to claim a GST credit on the benefit provided, then the tax effect is increased by the GST rate of 10 per cent. The individual top marginal rate of 47 per cent plus Medicare levy of 2 per cent plus the GST credit of 10 per cent gives us a nominal total of 59 per cent. The gross-up figure has to reflect this:

The gross amount of the payment is	238.60	(2.3860)
Less CGT credit of 10%	−21.69	(1/11th of the gross)
	216.91	
Less tax at the rate of 49% of the gross	−116.91	
Cash amount included in employee pay	100.00	

This is known as a Type 1 fringe benefit and will cover benefits such as payment of an employee's home electricity or telephone account, a meal, or tickets to a movie, concert or sporting event.

Therefore, if you provide a benefit to an employee worth $100 you have to gross it up by either 2.3860 if you were able to claim a GST credit on the benefit (FBT Type 1) or 1.9608 where no such GST credit can be claimed (FBT Type 2). Once grossed up you will arrive at a comparable pre-tax amount on which you will then pay your FBT at the 49 per cent rate that will apply to the 2015–2016 FBT year. It is this grossed-up amount that is included in the employee's employment summary as a reportable fringe benefit. *Note:* the above is for explanatory purposes only. Please refer to the current years' FBT guide for the correct uplift factors.

The fringe benefits tax you pay is an allowable tax deduction (FBT expense account). This is because it is something akin to wages and salaries and in the same category as PAYE deductions.

Therefore, the amount of FBT tax that must be paid on a $100 employee benefit for the 2016 FBT year is:

▶ for a Type 1 (GST credit) FBT benefit, 49 per cent of $238.60, or $116.91

▶ for a Type 2 (no GST) FBT benefit, 49 per cent of $196.08, or $96.08.

This calculation highlights why the FBT legislation is considered as imposing a penalty on businesses that provide a salary package of cash and benefits rather than just a cash amount. The one exception to this is motor vehicles, which is our next major discussion point.

A final note on FBT payments

These payments are deductible expenses to you the employer. But under the small business cash accounting rules the amount is deductible only when you actually pay it. Like other taxes, you will actually pay your FBT as a forward estimate on your BAS (or IAS, if you are not registered for the GST). When you lodge your annual FBT return the Tax Office will estimate your liability for your FBT for the next year and include that estimate on your BAS. However, this applies only if your FBT paid this year was in excess of $3000. You have to pay this 'estimate' even if your current year FBT liability is going to be less than $3000. You will get a refund of the excess when you lodge your annual return. If your current year FBT is going to be more than the estimate, you pay the estimate on your BAS and the difference with your annual return.

Reportable fringe benefits

Where the total FBT payments made to any employee exceed $2000 for the year, the employee's annual payment summary must contain the grossed-up amount as a *reportable fringe benefit*. This will not affect the employee's income tax liability, but it could affect any payments based on the employee's gross salary (child support payments, for example). *Note:* before 1 April 2007 the fringe benefits reporting exclusion threshold was $1000.

Tax rates

Please note that the tax rates, while current at the time of writing, are subject to change at the whim of the government. As the European Union has a VAT/GST minimum rate of 15 per cent, we in the industry all assumed that the initial 10 per cent GST rate would quickly rise to 12.5 per cent or 15 per cent. So far this has not happened, but the individual tax rates seem to change with every budget. For the latest rates please refer to the errata for this book on my website.

CHAPTER 8
Motor vehicles

Key areas we will cover in this chapter

▶ What is a car for fringe benefit purposes?

▶ How do you deduct your car expenses?

▶ Owner's cars

▶ Employee cars

▶ Methods of calculating the fringe benefit

▶ Disposals

Defined terms we will introduce

Car: for FBT purposes, a sedan, station wagon, four-wheel-drive vehicle, panel van, utility or any other vehicle with a carrying capacity of less than one tonne that has been designed to carry fewer than nine passengers

Private use: non-business use of a company-owned and-supplied vehicle

Substantiation: the method of claiming business use of a privately owned vehicle

There is hardly a business in Australia that does not use a motor vehicle of some kind. It is also the area that is 'greyest' in terms of what constitutes a motor vehicle and how to calculate private use compared to business use. Even the question of who owns the vehicle—the business or the business owner—is often not clear-cut. For these reasons this is a fairly complex area to deal with. This complexity is compounded if you consider that we must deal with three separate taxation concepts: income tax deductions, GST-creditable use and FBT liability, all of which must be in 'balance'—that is, you cannot claim a 50 per cent deduction for income tax and a one-third creditable use for GST purposes, but then in some cases you can and must! Confused? Let us try to demystify this very complex area.

In this chapter we are going to discuss the tax problems associated with motor vehicles. Under the tax laws, motor vehicles are divided squarely into two camps. There are the special purpose business vehicles that have very limited private use and there are all the others, mainly cars. A car is defined as a passenger vehicle designed to carry fewer than nine passengers and a load of less than one tonne. If you have a business vehicle that falls into this definition, for example a van of less than one tonne carrying capacity, then you must use the tax provisions that relate generally to cars. This also applies to business vehicles that are also used for private purposes. Let us firstly address the question of business vehicles.

Business vehicles

Cars have very specific tax laws associated with them, whereas other business vehicles that have a carrying capacity in excess of one tonne, such as utes and vans, are treated the same as any other business asset, provided the private use is minor or insignificant. However, certain commercial vehicles that would normally fall within this definition are also exempted provided they are used for work-related purposes and any private use is minor, infrequent or irregular. These include:

▶ taxis, panel vans and utilities

▶ other road vehicles designed to carry a load of less than one tonne but not designed to carry passengers

▶ unregistered cars for use in the business.

Home garaging of a business vehicle, by either the business owner or an employee, is acceptable and home-to-work transport is considered to be a business use for a special purpose business vehicle such as a trades van. It is considered that the van is available for business use at all times. On the other hand, vehicles that are treated as cars can also be home garaged but the home-to-business use is considered to be a private use.

If the business was to buy a computer you would work out the business versus private use and claim the business use portion of its purchase price as a tax deduction via depreciation (a capital allowance) and the business use portion of the GST credit. All expenses associated with the computer would also be handled in this fashion—that is, the expense would be split between the business use portion, which could be claimed as a tax deduction and the GST as a creditable acquisition, and the private use, which is not allowable under either tax regime. If your business was a registered company or a corporate trustee, then you could claim the full expenses associated with the computer and handle the private use portion under the FBT rules.

A business vehicle in excess of one tonne carrying capacity and with limited private use is handled in exactly the same way. When you sell it, say by trade-in, it is a taxable supply and the sale is subject to GST, or more technically a GST recoupment. You write off the asset in the normal manner without any further problems. If you are not registered for GST you can ignore the GST consequences of the purchase and ultimate sale.

At this stage we need to address a small point in regard to the GST and its *creditable use* rules. If your business is registered for GST and your business activity is a creditable activity, then the above applies. If you are not registered, you can ignore the GST implication, but if you are registered but engaged in the provision of input-taxed supplies, then you can claim only that proportion of your GST tax credit that relates to a creditable acquisition. Confused? If you run a business that is engaged 50 per cent in the provision of domestic rental accommodation (input taxed) and 50 per cent in construction (creditable), then you can claim only that 50 per cent of the GST that relates to your construction business as a creditable acquisition. This rule does not apply only to your business vehicles: it applies across the board to all of your asset purchases and expenses.

Cars

A 'car' is a passenger vehicle (excepting motorcycles but including four-wheel-drives, vans and the like) designed to carry fewer than nine passengers and a load of less than one tonne. A luxury car limit applies to such vehicles that limits the depreciation available and can trigger the 'luxury car tax'. This limit for 2014 is $57 466 and will be discussed later. A car also includes other business vehicles excluded from the treatment discussed above because of their private use component.

There are four broad sets of tax rules in regard to cars:

▶ *Cars owned by the business owners of a sole proprietorship or partnership.* If a sole proprietor or partner in a partnership owns a vehicle and uses it for work purposes, then the business expense of running the car can be claimed directly against the business. This is referred to as *substantiation*.

▶ *Cars owned by the business owners of a company or corporate trustee.* If the business is a company or a corporate trustee and it is the business that owns the vehicle, then any private use of that vehicle is subject to the FBT provisions. If the vehicle is a 'car' within the meaning of the FBT Act, then special provisions apply; otherwise any private use is covered by the residual benefits provisions.

▶ *Cars owned by an employee and used for business purposes.* If an employee owns a vehicle and uses it for work purposes, then the business expense of running the car can be claimed directly against the business using the substantiation rules.

▶ *Cars owned by the business and provided to the employee for business purposes.* If the business is a company or a corporate trustee and it is the business that owns the vehicle, then any private use of that vehicle by an employee is subject to the FBT provisions.

Motor vehicles that are 'cars' use substantiation

You can claim your car expenses either in your own personal tax return or against the business using the substantiation method if you own the vehicle as one of the following:

▶ a sole proprietor or a partner in a partnership

▶ the owner of a company where you own the vehicle and pay all the expenses

▶ an employee who uses their own vehicle for business purposes.

However, to make a claim that will allow for a GST credit, the claim must be made against the business itself. The first step is to determine which method you are going to use to calculate the deduction.

Where 'you' own the car, there are four ways to claim the business use proportion: cents per kilometre; one-third of actual expenses; 12 per cent of original value; and log book.

► *Cents per kilometre.* This is limited to 5000 business kilometres per year. Anything above this cannot be claimed under this method and may be 'lost'. You estimate your business kilometres for the period and multiply that by the approved rate per kilometre. The rates are available each year in the 'tax pack' (for example, the rate for a typical two-litre sedan in 2014 was 76c per kilometre). Log books are not required provided your estimate is reasonable in the circumstances, and you should be able to prove your estimate on some form of calculation basis (for example, once a day to the bank—52 weeks × 5 days [− 11 public holidays] at 10 km per round trip = 2490 km (to a max of 5000 km) @ 76c per km = $1892.40).

► *One-third of actual expenses.* If you can prove (by estimate or log book) that your business travel exceeds 5000 km per year and is in excess of one-third of the total kilometres driven, then you can claim one-third of the actual expenses such as registration, insurance, fuel, repairs, servicing, interest and depreciation for the year. You do not require any further proof of usage, but you need to be able to prove the expenses by invoice or other written documentation. Any excess business kilometres above one-third of the total kilometres will be lost under this option but you must travel at least one-third of the total kilometres for business purposes to use this option.

► *12 per cent of original value.* Again, if you exceed 5000 km of business use per year and your business travel is in excess of one-third of the total kilometres driven (by estimate or log book), you can claim your business expenses based on 12 per cent of the original value (or market value if the car is leased), up to the luxury car limit. No further substantiation, apart from proof of the original value, is required. Again, any excess business kilometres above one-third of the total will be lost under this option, but you must travel at least one-third of the total kilometres for business purposes to use this option.

▶ *Log book method*. This is the only method by which you can claim your actual expenses and is not limited to under or over the 5000 km mark. You must keep a log book for at least 12 continuous weeks in the first year to establish your business use as a percentage of your total kilometres travelled during the period. You then apply that percentage to the actual expenses for the period, including your depreciation expense. This process must be repeated every five years or if the vehicle is replaced. If you have more than one vehicle using the log book method, the same 12-week period must be used for each vehicle you own.

These methods may sound rather difficult but in practice are easily achieved provided the calculations are done on a regular basis. You must do the calculation for each car you wish to claim, although you can use a different method for each vehicle.

GST and substantiation

You can only claim the GST credit for the expense you actually incur and for which you have a tax invoice showing the GST amount. If the purchase is for an amount less than $82.50 (petrol, for instance), then just a simple receipt will do.

The amount you can claim depends on the method of substantiation you use. Firstly add up all of the GST amounts for the period, and then you can claim a percentage of that total as a GST credit in the GST paid account.

If you use the *cents per kilometre method* you can claim the percentage of your total GST credits set out in table 8.1.

Table 8.1: percentage of GST credits you can claim using cents per kilometre

Estimated kilometres travelled for a creditable purpose for a year	Assumed extent of creditable purpose (%)
0–1250	5
1251–2500	10
2501–3750	15
3751–5000	20

If you use either the *one-third of actual expenses* or the *12 per cent of original value method*, then you can claim 33⅓ per cent of your total GST credits (hence the need to prove the one-third use). If you use the *log book method* to determine your business kilometres, you can use the same percentage that you use for income tax to calculate the percentage of total GST credits you can claim.

As GST claims are usually made quarterly, it would be normal practice to make the motor vehicle claim on the business every quarter for GST purposes and accumulate the motor vehicle expense for income tax purposes at the end of the period.

If, as the business owner, you use your business funds to pay for all of the business expenses, then these would be recorded as a private expenditure against your drawings account (private motor vehicle expenses) and the drawings account would be partially offset each quarter against your quarterly motor vehicle claim. If your business is a company or corporate trustee, the drawings account would have to be settled before the end of the financial year or there could be adverse income tax and FBT implications. Let us look at an example (overleaf).

Claiming motor vehicle expenses for GST purposes—an example

Fred pays all of his motor vehicle expenses from his business account and makes a substantiation claim against the business on a quarterly basis. This quarter he paid $2000 for his motor vehicle, which he debits to his private motor vehicle account (an equity 'drawings' account). He then calculates that he has travelled 750 km this quarter for business purposes and makes a claim on the business at the appropriate rate, which in this case is 74c per km.

```
Dr   Motor vehicle expenses                 555
     Cr  Private motor vehicle expenses              555
Being the business kilometres for the
first quarter of 2014
```

The business kilometre claim is debited against an expense account (an allowable deduction against business income) and partially offsets the private motor vehicle expense (equity) account.

At 750 km per quarter, the annual kilometres travelled for business would be 3000 so the relevant GST claim percentage is 15 per cent. To calculate the gross GST paid for the quarter we divide the total expenses by 11 (2000 ÷ 11 = $181.18) and then apply the GST claim percentage to that amount ($181.18 × 15% = $27.27). We then journalise this amount into the GST liability account to be used to calculate our quarterly BAS liability:

```
Dr   GST liability                          27.27
     Cr  Private motor vehicle expenses              27.27
Being the quarterly GST creditable acquisition
for motor vehicle expenses
```

The GST paid on the business kilometres will be used to offset any GST collected from our business activities and will partially offset the private motor vehicle expense (equity) account.

Of course, any GST claim is subject to the *creditable purpose test* (it can't be an expenditure in regard to an input tax supply) and may have to be adjusted as the year progresses and your position becomes clearer.

Working out the FBT liability and 'contribution'

If your business is a registered company or corporate trustee and it is the business that owns the vehicle and you use it for private purposes, then you must account for the private use under the FBT rules.

You calculate the FBT owing on the private use and either register and pay the FBT calculated at the penalty rate or account for that private use through a 'contribution' of funds from your after-tax income. This could be achieved through a 'debit' to your drawings account that will then be included in your personal income in the form of salary (not salary sacrifice but from after-tax funds).

It is strongly suggested that, for cars incurring an FBT liability (vehicles owned by a company), you work out the FBT liability and then counter this with a 'contribution' in the form of a drawings account journal entry. This is far better than actually paying the FBT tax itself. In this way the business does not have to register for the FBT, nor do you have to fill in the annual FBT return and pay penalty tax on the calculated amount. It is referred to as the *contribution option*.

However, first we must determine the FBT amount of your private motor vehicle usage by one of two methods—the *statutory method* or the *operating costs method*. As the statutory method usually produces the best result it is the preferred method to use in most instances.

The statutory formula method

This method uses a statutory formula to determine the amount of the benefit received by the employee for the use of a fully maintained company car. The firm pays all of the expenses of owning the vehicle and claims the GST credits on all of those expenses. but the downside is that there is an assumed benefit to the employee for their private use of the vehicle.

The statutory method uses the 20 per cent of original value. This percentage was increased on 1 April 2014. Prior to this, lower percentages applied based on the kilometres travelled. For example, before this date it was 17 per cent for cars that travelled more than 40 000 km per year.

However, if you purchased the vehicle prior to 10 May 2011 the old kilometre-based rates still apply (see table 8.2).

Table 8.2: kilometre-based FBT rates using the statutory method

Kilometres travelled	% of private use
Less than 15 000	26
15 000–24 999	20
25 000–40 000	11
Greater than 40 000	7

You should note that under this formula you must use the statutory percentage based on the annualised kilometres. What this means is the actual kilometres for cars that you have owned for the full year, or what the vehicle would have travelled based on actual kilometres as if you had owned it for the full year. If you own a car for six months and it has done 26 000 km, its annualised kilometres would be double that at 52 000 and the statutory formula you apply would be 7 per cent, not the 11 per cent that would apply to a 26 000 km annual amount.

Having determined your percentage rate, the next step in calculating your private use amount is to determine the base value of the vehicle. This is its original GST-inclusive cost including any accessories, and on-road without any allowance given for depreciation. If you have owned or leased the vehicle for more than four years at the start of the FBT year, then the 'cost' is reduced by one-third.

You now multiply the cost by the percentage to get the dollar amount of private use irrespective of the vehicle's actual business use. This is the amount of the benefit provided to the employee and is now treated the same as any other fringe benefit amount using the appropriate uplift to get the gross amount and the fringe benefits tax percentage to determine the amount payable.

Of course, the amount payable is reduced by any amount contributed by the employee out of after-tax funds that offsets the statutory fringe benefit amount as we have calculated. The contributed funds can include any amount that the employee spends on running or maintaining the vehicle, such as privately purchased petrol.

The statutory method can in some instances be very generous, as in the case of a spouse using a company car where they have very little business use. For this reason various governments have tried to remove this concession, but so far the business lobby has prevailed.

The operating cost method

This method works in a fashion similar to the substantiation log book method in so far as you keep a log book of your business mileage to determine the private use percentage and then apply that to the motor vehicle expenses to determine the private contribution amount. If the statutory formula gives a better result you must use that. *Note:* in working out the amount payable under the operating cost method you must use a depreciation amount of 25 per cent rather than any rate worked out under the capital allowances or small business concessions.

There are two steps in determining the private use benefit under the operating cost method.

Firstly, you must determine all of the GST-inclusive operating costs of the car during the FBT year, such as:

▶ petrol

▶ registration and insurance

▶ repairs and maintenance

▶ if the car is owned, depreciation on the GST-inclusive cost using the written-down value at 25 per cent rate

▶ if the car is owned, the notional interest on the GST-inclusive opening written-down value of the car at 6.45 per cent (for the 2014 FBT year) of the opening value (irrespective of the actual interest rate, if any)

▶ if the car is leased, the annual lease payments.

Step 2 is to determine the private use percentage. This is normally done using a log book, which is only required to be kept for 12 continuous weeks every four years. The private use percentage is calculated using the log book record of business kilometres travelled compared to the total kilometres for the log book period. Each car requires its own log book. You keep a record of the total kilometres travelled each year by each car the business owns.

You calculate the car benefit by multiplying the total operating cost by the private use percentage. As in the substantiation method, this benefit can be reduced by any private expenditure on the car or any amount contributed to the business from after-tax funds that are intended to offset the private use.

The fringe benefit is then grossed up in the normal way and the fringe benefit tax calculated using the fringe benefit tax percentage.

Luxury cars

If the initial purchase price of a car, as defined earlier, exceeds the 'luxury car' value for the year, then any depreciation allowable on that vehicle is limited to the luxury car limit, as is any GST credit.

With the exception of genuine short-term (less than one month) hire contracts, all luxury car leases are treated as purchases. That is, the lease is treated as a loan, where only the finance charge (interest, fees and so on) portion of the loan is deductible, and the purchase price is subject to depreciation up to the car limit. The finance charge and the depreciation claimed must be adjusted for private use, as already discussed.

Note that if you purchase a luxury car you will be taxed at a rate of 33 per cent on the excess over and above the car limit after deducting the full GST credit. The luxury car tax is paid by your motor vehicle supplier.

The luxury car tax is one of the many government support mechanisms for the car industry in Australia. Now that Holden and Ford have indicated they will no longer be manufacturing cars in Australia the tax may be revised.

Disposal of the motor vehicle

When it comes to selling the motor vehicle, the treatment varies according to who has claimed ownership of the vehicle and the method used to account for private use. There is also the added complexity of GST for those taxpayers who are registered for GST purposes.

Balancing charge event

The term *balancing charge* refers to the final depreciation calculation that is made when you dispose of a vehicle. If you claimed too much depreciation against your income you must pay it back—it is classed as income; if you claimed too little it is an expense.

If you 'leased' the vehicle and did not claim any depreciation for it but only the lease payments in full, then no balancing charge event is applicable—it applies only to 'owned' vehicles where an amount of depreciation was claimed. However, the tax law in regard to lease payments applies only to situations where you do not intend to purchase the vehicle and the purchase price is under the luxury car limit. If you pass-in the vehicle then you will be within the law; however, if you purchase and then resell the vehicle at the end of the lease period you could find that you must determine the appropriate adjustment and include that in your tax return. You should seek professional advice if you find yourself in this situation.

Balancing charge event using substantiation

If you own the vehicle and pay all expenses from your private funds and then claim for business use on the business, the disposal of the motor vehicle is a private matter.

If you use the substantiation method to claim your business use, and you have only ever used the cents per kilometre or the 12 per cent of original cost method, then there is no balancing charge required on disposal.

If you used the one-third of expenses method or the log book method to determine the percentage of expense claimed, or a mixture of all four methods, and then claimed this against your personal income tax, there would be a balancing charge to be worked out.

If you are a sole trader, and you have been paying all of the expenses from your business funds, and adjusting those claims according to the substantiation rules—that is, you were just claiming the business proportion as if you were a private individual claiming motor vehicle expenses according to substantiation—then the *balancing charge* is included in your tax return as part of your business expenses or income (it can be positive).

Balancing adjustment on disposal

Where a company owns a vehicle and then disposes of that vehicle, a balancing adjustment will be required. We have already discussed this concept in chapter 4. The disposal of a motor vehicle is handled in exactly the same way as the disposal of any other business asset.

Sales versus trade-in

Whether you sold the vehicle, traded it in or just gave it to your son, you handle the disposal in the same manner. In the case of a trade-in the 'money received' does not go into the bank but rather is debited to the asset account of the new vehicle to bring its purchase price up to its full value for depreciation purposes. If you dispose of it to a related party the 'funds received' will have to be based on the market value of the vehicle disposed of.

GST on disposal

If you are registered for the GST and you sell or trade in a business vehicle, then you can (indeed must) treat this as a taxable supply. That is, you have sold a GST-able asset. You provide the dealer with a tax invoice for the sale price, or the agreed amount of the trade-in, and include GST as 1/11th of the value on the invoice. You then account for this as a taxable supply—that is, a sale with a GST amount included. The sale of all business assets on which you have claimed a GST credit must be treated in this manner. If you have a private use component, you can adjust the GST amount so that it represents the business proportion of the sale.

Pro-forma tax invoice

Agreed value for trade-in		$2100
Private proportion of vehicle (estimated at 50%)	$1000	
Business proportion	$1000	
GST on business proportion	$ 100	

When working out any balancing charge amounts, the value of the 'sale' for these purposes is the net value less the GST amount.

Leasing, rentals and hire purchase by companies

If you are *purchasing* the vehicle through any of these methods, then you record the transaction as a purchase — that is, you create an asset account for the vehicle and a loan account for the obligation. Any GST credit or borrowing expense is claimed over the period of the loan agreement and the asset is depreciated in the normal manner, as discussed in chapter 4. Only the interest charge of the lease, hire purchase or loan repayments is deductible.

Cars for employees

As an employer, you have four options when providing cars for business use by employees:

▶ Allow the employee to claim business use of their own private vehicle against the company when it is used for business purposes. This can be at any agreed (although reasonable) rate but it is usual for such claims to be based on the substantiation rules. The employee includes the amount claimed as income in their individual tax return (the amount is included in their annual tax payment summary) and claims the business use through the substantiation provisions. The claim you pay them is simply an expense to the company and treated as a reimbursement of employee expenses.

▶ Give the employee an allowance as part of their salary package, possibly including a petrol allowance as well. *This is the preferred method for small businesses.* The allowance is part of the employee's salary package and is again included as income to the employee, with the employee able to claim business use on their own tax returns via the substantiation method.

▶ You can provide a car that is to be used strictly only for business purposes, with no private use permitted. With the exception of delivery-type vehicles, no travel to or from work or overnight home garaging is permitted. Usually such an arrangement is not applicable to small businesses and is the province of large corporations running pool cars. The only exception is for vehicles such as delivery-type vans that should be kept under very tight control to ensure no unauthorised private use is undertaken.

▶ The business pays for a motor vehicle, which is then 'given' to the employee to be used for business purposes. Fringe benefits are payable by the employer on the private use of such a vehicle and any contribution by the employee. If this option is used then professional assistance should be sought in order to determine the tax effect of such an arrangement.

In summary, where a 'car' in the normal sense is required for use by employees for business purposes, the business use expenses of that car should be provided as an allowance. The allowance can be as generous as the employer wishes and can cover such things as vehicle repayments and maintenance, as well as an allowance based on business mileage undertaken. Motor charge cards in the employer's or employee's name can also be used provided the employee is ultimately responsible for any expenses on the card that are not included in the allowance.

Note: All employee allowances and reimbursements should (must) be paid through their salary. If you pay on a claim direct, say by cheque, it could be considered to fall within the withholding tax provisions, which would require you to withhold 49 per cent of the payment. Under the salary provisions the employee could elect to have the allowance paid 'tax free' (a *tax variation*, in formal terms) as it is subject to a tax deduction in their hands.

In the case of commercial delivery vans and the like, these can be provided strictly on a business use basis, but can be home garaged and used for personal transport to and from work without incurring an FBT liability provided that the travel is incidental to the business use of the vehicle (such as deliveries made on the way home or to work).

CHAPTER 9

Goods and services tax (GST)

Key areas we will cover in this chapter

▶ Registering for the GST

▶ Business expenses

▶ Sales

▶ GST classifications

▶ Tax invoices

▶ Paying the GST

▶ Annual returns

▶ Correcting mistakes

▶ GST-free sales

▶ Tax input sales

▶ GST credits

▶ GST accounting

▶ The simplified accounting method (SAM)

Defined terms we will introduce

You: in GST terms means you as a business, a sole trader, a partnership, a trustee of a trust or a company

Enterprise: has the same meaning as business

Annual turnover: has the same meaning as aggregate turnover as used in the small business concessions

Aggregated turnover: the annual turnover of all of your associated businesses

GST turnover: the turnover of your business as a single entity without reference to your associated businesses; does not include asset disposals

Taxable supplies: has the same meaning as sales

Acquisitions: has the same meaning as purchases

Consideration: has the same meaning as payment (given or received)

Input tax credit: has the same meaning as GST credit

Micro business: a small business with an annual turnover under $2 million

If your annual business turnover, or anticipated turnover, is in excess of $75 000 ($150 000 for non-profit organisations), then you must register for the GST. You must also register for the GST if you run a taxi business, irrespective of your turnover. You can do this when you register your business for an ABN or at any time through the business entry point at www.business.gov.au, but once registered you must stay registered for at least 12 months.

If you are *not* registered for the GST

If you are under this turnover limit then you can safely ignore the GST, although you must still quote your ABN on all your 'tax invoices' and ensure you indicate that no GST is payable on your sales or services. This means that neither you nor your customers can claim the GST credits, nor are you liable for any GST on your sales.

When you sell an item (or invoice for your services) there is no GST included in that amount. This means you account for the whole amount in your accounts as a sale. But it also means your client is unable to claim any GST paid on their purchase. When you purchase an item, or pay an expense, you account for the whole amount without any deduction for the GST component. You will not have to fill in any GST amounts on your IAS or make any GST payments to the ATO.

You should also supply a tax invoice with every sale. The tax invoice should include your business name, address, ABN and words to the effect that there is no GST included in the cost.

A business that can't claim the GST from your supply perhaps could from your competitors, and you may lose sales because of this. Some companies under the limit still register for the GST for this reason.

If you are registered for the GST

Some items, such as basic food, financial arrangements and some government charges, are exempt from the GST. Practically everything else you purchase is subject to the GST and you can claim a GST credit on that purchase provided that:

▶ you have a valid tax invoice for the purchase, and

▶ the amount of the invoice either indicates that it is GST inclusive or shows the amount of the GST included.

The amount of GST you can claim is either the amount of GST shown or 1/11th of the invoice total if the GST amount is not shown.

Business expense

You claim the GST credit for all your business purchases including your trading stock, your depreciable assets and your expenses. However, you only take up into your accounting records the net cost of the purchase exclusive of the GST. For example, if you buy a computer system for $3300, the computer system would show in your records for depreciation purposes at a cost of $3000, with the $300 GST being debited to your GST account. The same applies to stock purchases and other expenses.

In an accounting system such as MYOB you just enter the full amount with the GST code and the system will break up the expense into the GST component and the net amount that it will debit to the appropriate expense or asset code.

If you make a purchase that you are going to use for both private and business purposes, you must claim the GST credit only in proportion to your estimated business use. Refer to chapter 3 for a more detailed explanation.

Sales

When you make a sale you include in the invoice total both the amount of the sale and the amount of the GST, 10 per cent of the sale value. In tax terms the GST is 1/11th of the sale price whether or not you made this calculation. 'Whoops, I forgot!' is not an excuse. If you are registered for the GST *all* of your sales include GST.

In entering the sales into your records you will include 1/11th of the sales value in the GST account and the remaining 10/11ths in the sales account.

Again, in MYOB you simply enter the full amount with the GST code and the system will break up the sales income into the GST component and the net amount that it will credit to the sales account.

What is a sale? The correct term is a *taxable supply*. It not only includes sales in the traditional sense but also goods you hire out and any disposals of business assets on which you have claimed a GST credit (a trade-in, for example).

If you have used an asset you dispose of for both private and business use, you 'charge' GST only on the business use.

Some 'supplies' are GST free, the main one being basic food items. A problem can arise if you sell both GST-free and GST-able goods; in this case you must break up your receipts accordingly, or you may use the ATO proportions method instead. These accepted percentages are listed at the end of this chapter.

Some 'supplies' are input taxed. The most common example is residential rent (not commercial, but a house or flat). In this case you do not return any GST on the rent, but you also cannot claim any GST credits on purchases made in relation to the house or flat. Caravan parks also fall into this category in relation to long-term residents.

GST classifications

When you record your income or expenses you will have to 'classify' them for GST purposes. Mostly your entry will be subject to the GST and therefore classifies as 'GST', but expense items such as interest (financial supplies) have no GST and therefore will be classified as 'N-T' (No Tax).

If you classify an income or expense as 'GST'—that is, the amount is subject to the GST—then the system will take 1/11th of the amount entered and apply that to the correct GST account and the remainder to the selected account code. This automates the procedure to a great extent.

Tax invoices

You should supply a 'tax invoice' for every sale or supply. Your standard invoices should be pre-printed to include the words 'Tax Invoice', your business name, address and ABN. When creating the invoice you include the date, details of the goods, their tax-inclusive (full) price and the amount of GST included in the price (or a statement to the effect that the total price includes the GST). If the sale is for over $1000 you must also include the name of your customer and their address and/or ABN.

Till receipts can be tax invoices if they meet the above criteria. Usually till receipts do not include the name and address of your client and therefore are only valid for sales under $1000.

If your sale includes both taxable and non-taxable items, as in the example of basic food and other items, then you must indicate the taxable and non-taxable items and the total GST included in the sale. In the case of a deli selling to the public at large, you will not normally issue a tax invoice as such, but you must be prepared to issue one on request.

Paying the GST

You must pay your GST on your BAS (Business Activity Statement), which you will receive, partly completed, each quarter from the Tax Office. You must complete the BAS even if your GST sales and expenses are zero. (*Hint:* zero means 0, not nil—BAS forms are scanned and the system does not recognise nil as 0.)

If you are accounting for your income tax and your GST on a cash basis—that is, you are what the ATO refers to as a small business and we refer to as a micro business—this means you include the GST on your purchases and sales when you actually are paid or pay the accounts. You do not include any credit purchases or sales on your BAS return. But remember, you must have a tax invoice before you can claim any GST credits.

If your GST turnover is in excess of $20 million, you must report and pay your GST monthly and lodge your activity statement electronically.

If your turnover is below this amount, then you have three payment options:

1   Report and pay your actual GST quarterly.

2   Pay your actual GST quarterly but include limited information and then make an annual information report.

3   If your turnover is under $20 million, you can elect to pay a quarterly instalment calculated by the Tax Office and fill in an annual GST return.

For the sake of simplicity, however, most small businesses account for the GST on a quarterly BAS.

You must complete your BAS by the 28th day of the month after the quarter. But this requires that you submit it to the Tax Office by the 28th day, which means you have very limited time to fill in the BAS, and it is for this reason that the Tax Office allows the BAS to be completed on-line.

If you are a micro business and wish to use the third option, you must lodge at least two BAS statements that calculate your actual GST liability before you can elect to convert over to the instalment method. The Tax Office will advise you on your quarterly BAS when you are eligible to take up this option and will have the instalment amounts pre-printed on the form.

Although the instalment option is considered the easiest, it is not necessarily the best option for most taxpayers. Once you elect to use the instalment option you are locked in for that year. If you vary the instalments and make a mistake you can be subject to a penalty, and if you are owed a refund you will receive this only when you fill in the annual return. Basically, if the instalments are close to or less than your true GST liability and you do not expect a refund, then use the instalment system; otherwise use option 1 and complete the full BAS using the 'accounts' method—that is, just complete the GST amounts paid and received directly from your accounts.

The easiest method to pay your BAS is at a post office using the BAS payment advice. You can also pay electronically via direct debit or BPAY, or by mailing a cheque along with your completed BAS form.

After making the payment you must forward the BAS form to the Tax Office at the address printed on the form.

Annual returns

If you elect to use option 2, the GST estimate or option 3 the instalment method, the Tax Office you will send you an annual GST return. On this return you include the actual GST collected and GST paid for the year as well as your total sales, expenses and capital acquisitions. This return must be lodged by the time you lodge your income tax return or at the latest by 28 February of the following year. That gives you at least five months to complete the annual processing and lodge the return. All the information should be readily available from the annual accounts you have printed out from your accounting system.

Correcting mistakes

Occasionally a situation will arise that will alter the amount of GST you should have paid for the period, such as a change in the price you are to pay or receive, the cancellation of a transaction or recovery of a bad debt.

In these cases, if you use the instalment/annual return option, then provided that your error is less than $5000 you can make the correction on the next annual return. If you use option 1 and fill in a complete BAS each quarter, you can correct the error up to 18 months after you find it and on the 'current' BAS. Just correct the GST paid or GST collected amounts accordingly.

If the error is greater than $5000 you will have to correct the BAS involved—either the annual BAS for instalment taxpayers or the appropriate quarterly BAS for option 1 taxpayers.

GST-free sales

If you make a sale that is 'connected with Australia', then it is a taxable sale and you must return 1/11th of the sales value as a GST receipt. If the sale is not connected with Australia—that is, it is an export transaction—then it is a GST-free sale and there is no GST included in that sale.

There are a number of sales that are GST free, including:

- most basic food
- some education courses
- some medical, health and care services
- some medical aids and appliances
- some medicines
- most exports
- some childcare
- some religious services
- water, sewerage and drainage
- international transport
- precious metals (such as gold)
- inwards duty free
- farmland
- international mail.

You do not include any GST in the sales value and you can claim the GST credits for inputs into these supplies.

The sale of a business as a going concern is also GST-free if:

- everything that makes the business a going concern is included
- the seller carries on the business until the day it is sold
- before the sale the buyer and the seller agree in writing that the sale is of a going concern.

Input-taxed sales

Similar to GST-free, you do not include GST in the sale price of these goods but unlike GST-free, in the case of input taxed sales you cannot claim the GST credits on inputs related to the supply—hence the term *input taxed*. Input taxed supplies fall into two main categories, financial supplies and residential rent, but not commercial rent.

Input-taxed financial supplies cover a wide variety of situations and occur when you do any of the following:

► Lend or borrow money.

► Grant credit to a customer.

► Buy or sell shares or other securities.

► Provide or receive credit under a hire purchase agreement in which the credit is disclosed.

Tax invoices

A purchase under $82.50 does not require a tax invoice; a simple receipt will suffice. A sale over this amount must be accompanied by a tax invoice that includes the following information:

► the descriptor 'Tax Invoice'

► the seller's name, address and ABN

► the date of the invoice

► a brief description of the goods sold

► the amount of the GST included, as either a line item or a note, and if it is a mixed supply an indication of what items are taxable and what are GST-free.

If the sale is over $1000 the invoice must also include the purchaser's name and address.

I have used the word *must*, but the law requires only that a tax invoice be produced on demand; the *must* refers to the commercial reality of the situation.

GST credits

If you are registered for the GST then you can claim a credit against the GST you collected on your sales (that is, payable to the Tax Office) with the GST you yourself paid on your purchases. You should note, however, that the term *sales* is not used in the accounting sense of sales in the normal course of business but rather anything you dispose of in the course of business, including sales of stock or disposals of company assets. Purchases likewise include purchases of stock but also any other acquisitions.

So the GST on the total disposals you make during the period can be offset with the GST you paid on the total acquisitions you made during the period. This is different from accounting, where trading stock sales and trading stock purchases are accounted for immediately but asset acquisitions are accounted for over time in the form of depreciation. The GST knows nothing about amortisation—everything is immediate!

You can claim a credit provided the acquisition was for use in the business. If it was private then no credit is available, and if it was only part business then only that part is creditable. And of course you must have a tax invoice from your supplier and that supplier must themselves be registered for the GST. Purchases from a non-registered entity carry no GST credit.

If your tax invoice does not specifically stipulate the amount of GST included in the acquisition, then you can calculate this by dividing the purchase price by 1/11th (not 10 per cent). For example, a good costing $100 will attract a 10 per cent GST, making the purchase price to you $110, of which 1/11th is the GST—that is, $10.00.

Not everything is GST creditable, however. Some of the main exclusions are:

▶ financial supplies such as interest paid

▶ goods or services purchased for which you cannot claim a tax deduction (for example, entertainment expenses)

▶ motor vehicles (capped by the luxury car limit)

▶ public utilities such as gas, water and council rates.

There are other special rules that apply to pre-establishment costs, second-hand purchases, periodic payments such as leases, lay-by purchases and purchases made with corporate credit cards.

GST accounting

If you have a turnover of less than $2 million and report your income tax on a cash basis (a micro business), then you can also account for your GST on a cash basis. Essentially this means your GST payments and GST credits are all accounted for when you actually settle the account and not when the account was first presented. Under cash accounting you will never have a bad debt for either income tax or GST purposes.

If you account for your GST on an accruals basis (normal accounting methodology) then you pay your GST and claim the GST credits when the liability is past, in normal business when you send or receive the invoice. Under accrual accounting you may encounter bad debts and have to adjust your GST paid accordingly.

Simplified accounting method (SAM) for food retailers

If you are registered for the GST you must account for the GST separately from your income and expenses. For businesses that have both GST-payable and GST-free purchases and sales, such as the corner deli, this can be a problem. The Tax Office has created simplified accounting methods for food retailers. A booklet titled 'Simplified GST accounting methods' is available from the ATO website or from its help line. If you are a food retailer you should obtain a copy of this guide.

However, the simplified method is only available for food retailers who are registered for the GST and have a turnover under $2 million, whether or not they use the cash accounting method.

The special rules in overview

The basic problem is that a deli will sell both basic foodstuffs that are GST-free and other items that are subject to the GST. All are usually sold on the one account, often under $82.50 and not requiring a formal GST receipt. Where your sales terminal can distinguish between the sales, for example with a barcode reader, there is not a problem; the problem normally arises in outlets that rely on the traditional till.

There are five methods that you may use to determine your GST-free and GST-payable sales mix:

▶ the business norms method

▶ the stock purchases method

▶ the snapshot method

- ▶ sales percentage
- ▶ purchases snapshot.

Which method you can use will depend on the type of business you run. If you just purchase and sell products, then you can use any method; however, if you 'convert' your purchases into something else (for instance, you buy potatoes and sell hot chips), then you cannot use the stock purchase method, and you can use the sales percentage method only if your converted food makes up less than 5 per cent of your sales.

The business norms method—available to all food retailers

Basically this method allows you to apply a fixed percentage to your purchases and sales (ignoring the actual GST) to distinguish between GST-payable and GST-free purchases and sales rather than the actual GST amounts. For example, if your business is a delicatessen that does not sell hot food or prepared meals, you can classify 90 per cent of your purchases and 85 per cent of your sales as GST free (see table 9.1).

Table 9.1: fixed percentages for sales and purchases—the business norms method

Business	% GST-free sales	% GST-free purchases
Cake shop	2	95
Continental deli that does not sell hot or prepared meals	85	90
Convenience stores that prepare takeaway food	22.5	30
Fresh fish retailers that mainly retail fresh fish with some cooked fish	35	98
Health food shops that do not convert GST-free food into taxable food	35	98
Hot bread shops	50	75
Pharmacy with both taxable and GST-free food sales: – Dispensary (non-claimable) – Over the counter	 98 47.5	 Nil 2
Rural convenience stores that may include sales of fuel or Australia Post agencies: – Converter – Non-converters	 22.5 30	 30 30

A food retailer is anyone who sells both prepared (GST-payable) and basic (GST-free) food, such as a cake shop, delicatessen, hot bread shop or health food shop or a pharmacy that sells food.

The stock purchases method — not available to food converters

This method is available only to businesses that do not convert GST-free food into GST-taxable food. In other words, you sell your stock as you receive it, other than perhaps repackaging.

Basically this method again allows you to apply the same fixed percentage to both your purchases and your sales (ignoring the actual GST) to distinguish between GST-payable and GST-free purchases and sales rather than the actual GST amounts. However, rather than a Tax Office percentage, you work out the percentage yourself by examining your purchases over a four-week period and applying this percentage to both purchases and sales. You must do this at least twice a year to account for seasonal fluctuations. If you estimate that your GST-free sales are less than 5 per cent of your total sales, you need only track the GST-free purchases over the two four-week periods.

Alternatively you can use your actual GST-free purchases if your system of stock control allows for this.

The snapshot method — available to all food retailers

This method is similar to the stock purchases method, except that you sample both your purchases and your sales and then apply appropriate percentages to each.

The sales percentage method — available only if your conversion is less than 5 per cent

This method is designed for supermarkets or convenience stores that are almost exclusively resellers and have adequate point-of-sale (POS) equipment. Under this method you determine your GST-free sales for the GST period (quarter) from your POS system and apply this percentage to your purchases.

The purchases snapshot method—available to all food retailers

This method applies only to your stock purchases; you must work out your GST liability on sales from your POS system. Under this method you sample your purchases twice a year for a period of four weeks each and then apply the percentage of GST-free purchases to your purchases for the whole year.

Notifying the Tax Office

If you wish to use the simplified accounting method you must fill in an election form available from the ATO website and lodge it with the Tax Office. You will then be committed to using this method for at least 12 months.

CHAPTER 10
Putting it all together

Key areas we will cover in this chapter

▶ Tax accounting

▶ End of period processing

Defined term we will introduce

Tax accounting: keeping your business records in such a manner that they satisfy the Tax Office requirements

Trial Balance: an accounting report that lists the closing balance of all accounts for the period, used to prove all entries have balanced. Considered to be the end-point of the bookkeeping process.

Franking credit: the amount of tax paid by the company on the income they pay as a dividend to you, which you can then use as a tax credit. Also known by the terms *imputation credits* and *dividend streaming*

When we first go into business for ourselves we are often amazed by the amount of paperwork involved in meeting our obligations, especially in relation to taxation. Of course, we do not keep records just to satisfy taxation requirements, but our main accounting system (MYOB, for example) is usually exclusively for that purpose. Other records, such as scheduling, quoting and job costing, are usually kept separate from our main system, often in the form of Excel spreadsheets, leaving our computerised accounting system as the main medium for satisfying our taxation requirements. The question we will attempt to answer in this chapter is this: how do we use our accounting system to best achieve this result?

Tax accounting

Your accounting system will categorise your business transactions under a number of headings. This is called a chart of accounts and is standard across all accounting systems worldwide (although the method of numbering or identifying individual accounts within the system will vary form one system to another):

1 Assets

- ► Current assets

- ► Long-term assets

- ► Intangible assets

2 Liabilities

- ► Current liabilities

- ► Long-term liabilities

3 Equity

- ► Capital

- ► Drawings

- ► Retained earnings

4 Income

5 Cost of sales

6 Expenses

7 Other income

8 Other expenses.

Unlike large businesses, which must conform to the International Accounting Standards, small and medium businesses keep their accounts primarily to satisfy the taxman and therefore keep their records according to the Tax Act as it applies to them at the time. We have discussed this legislation in some depth in previous chapters but now is the time to look at how to put this into practice!

The reason we must be careful how we treat our business income and expenses is that our BAS will be produced from the information we capture in our system, and our income tax return will be completed from the details shown on our trial balance. To ensure that our trial balance displays the correct information we must be very careful how we record that information in the first instance.

To that end we must first look to the two classifications of 'Other'. If the income item is not income in the normal course of business it must be classified as 'Other Income', and if an expense is not an allowable deduction it must be classified as 'Other deduction'. It is these 'Other' amounts that will require special treatment when we complete our tax return. Completed correctly, a good set of books will minimise your accountancy costs; completed badly and your accountant will have to reconstruct the accounts, which will cost you dearly!

You should also be aware that the Other classifications are used for income or expenses that have been incurred outside the normal course of business. Only business income or business expenses incurred in the normal course of your business activities should be included in your income or expense classifications.

Expense or asset?

If you spend less than $100 it is an expense. If you spend more than $1000 on an asset, however, you must classify the amount as an asset and create an asset account specifically for that item. If you are a micro business — that is, one that has a turnover of less than $2 million — then you depreciate the asset at 15 per cent for the first year and then 30 per cent after that (known as the *small business 'pool' rate*); otherwise you depreciate the asset over its effective life. This was discussed in chapter 4, on capital allowances.

If you expend money on an asset that is under $1000, then:

▶ as a micro business you are able to claim that amount as an expense and add it to an expense account called 'Low Cost Assets'

▶ as a small business that has a turnover of more than $2 million you must add this amount to an asset account called 'Low Value Assets' and depreciate it at the rate of 18.75 per cent for the first year and 37.5 per cent for subsequent years, based on the reducing value method.

Is the expense deductible?

In chapter 3, on taxable income and allowable deductions, we discussed what was an allowable deduction to the business. In the accounting sense, allowable deductions equate to expenses. However, legitimate business expenses that are not allowable as a taxation deduction, such as entertainment expenses, should be classified as an Other Expense amount.

In chapter 4 we also discussed the balancing charge that occurs when we dispose of an asset. Although the balancing charge is an allowable deduction, we should also classify it as an Other Expense (or Other Income, if it is positive), because it is not an expense incurred in the normal course of business and including such an expense in our expense classification (or income classification, if positive) will adversely affect our budget outcomes.

Is it income from business activities or not?

Our income classification should only include income from normal business activities that is classified as 'Assessable Income' for income tax purposes. Apart from the balancing charge event discussed above, the other prime candidate for the Other Income classification is interest. Although it is an assessable income amount, it is an amount of income generated not from normal business activities but rather from investment activities, and is therefore classified as an Other amount to ensure it does not adversely affect our budget outcomes by overstating our income from operations. It should also be noted that interest expense is considered to be a cost of doing business and is therefore classified as a normal expense rather than as an Other Expense.

End-of-period processing

There are special requirements that a business must meet on a weekly, monthly, quarterly and annual basis. These functions are cumulative — that is, you must still do your weekly processing along with, or preferably before, your monthly ones. Similarly you must do your monthly activities before you undertake your quarterly ones, and so on.

Your weekly activities must be done *every* week. In addition, your monthly activities must be completed *every* month and your quarterly activities *every* quarter. Your annual activities are usually undertaken well after the end of the financial year and after all other processing is complete.

Weekly

Your accounting records should be kept up to date on a regular basis. Every week you should ensure that all of your receipts are deposited into your bank account and all of your transactions, deposits and expenses, whether by cheque, credit card or direct debit, are recorded. Be sure to classify your expenses accurately as either the purchase of an asset or a revenue expense, and ensure that the proper treatment is accorded to expense items that contain an element of personal use. You should also print a trial balance and a set of accounts after you have completed this task just to keep abreast of how your business is progressing, especially in relation to cash flow. The big question to always keep in mind is, 'Do I have enough cash to meet my estimated future expenses?'

Monthly

Your business must have its own bank accounts and, if necessary, its own credit card account (for business expenses). You should also ensure that statements of these accounts are made available to you on a monthly basis. Fortunately most statements are now available via the internet and can be monitored every week but you should still print out a formal monthly statement for your records.

Bank Reconciliation Statement

Each month you must reconcile the account balances in your books with the statement balances. You must do this for all accounts, including cheque, credit card and loan accounts. This process is known as a Bank Reconciliation Statement and this report should be filed with your monthly bank statement.

Monthly Income Activity Statement—PAYG withholding

For most small businesses that employ staff, you will pay the income tax you have withheld from your employees' salaries and wages to the Tax Office on a quarterly basis. However, if your annual withholding amount exceeds $25 000 then this will result in an income activity statement being sent out each month. Refer to the quarterly processing section for details of the information required.

Quarterly

For most small businesses the quarterly processing requirements are the most onerous; however, if you have already completed your bank reconciliations on a monthly basis as suggested above, then the quarterly requirements can be handled quite easily within the specified timeframe imposed by the BAS, usually 28 days after the end of the quarter.

Superannuation

For businesses that employ staff, you must deposit into your employees' superannuation account the amount of the compulsory superannuation guarantee. You must do this at least quarterly and both keep a written record of the payment and inform your staff member in writing detailing the payment.

Loan repayments

When you repay a loan, you can only claim the non-capital component (Interest) as a deduction against your income. In plain English, when you make the loan repayments, debit them against your loan principal in your liabilities account. Ask your loan provider (bank) to send you a loan statement at least quarterly. When you receive this, compare the balance on the statement with your account balance and make the necessary journal entry that credits the loan account and debits the loan expenses (Interest paid) with the difference. That difference is the amount of fees, interest and other expenses the bank has charged you for the period. The GST code is 'N-T', as these are non-taxable amounts.

Personal use — motor vehicles

On a quarterly basis, you should determine the amounts that are owed to you or that you owe the business in relation to business use versus private use of your motor vehicle. If you are satisfying your FBT liabilities by the contribution method, you should transfer this amount into the business from your after-tax funds or source them from your drawings account, where such funds are to be converted into salary and tax paid accordingly. Chapter 7, on fringe benefits tax, discussed this in some detail.

Quarterly BAS

Each quarter you will receive a BAS, if you are registered for the GST, or an IAS if you are not. We will use the term BAS loosely to include both, as the difference from a business viewpoint is minimal.

The form may include printed Tax Office estimates of your income tax liability, your FBT liability (if applicable) and perhaps your GST if you elect the annual option. You would normally just accept the Tax Office estimates in regard to these amounts.

There are potentially four taxes paid on your quarterly BAS:

▶ GST (if you are registered)

▶ PAYG instalment (income tax instalment for sole traders or companies)

▶ PAYG withholding (the amounts you have withheld from employee wages)

▶ fringe benefits tax (if you lodged an FBT return for last year).

It should be noted at this point that if you decide not to use the Tax Office estimates and as a result you underpay your tax liability, you could incur a penalty. However, if you accept the Tax Office estimates and this results in an underpayment, no fine or penalty is imposed.

As a small business you would normally have to complete the BAS every quarter, working out your GST liability and including any amounts that you have withheld from employee wages. If you have any problems with this process, refer to the BAS chapter in my book *Learn Bookkeeping in 7 Days*, which explains how to account for the GST.

Annual

Here I am referring to the end of the financial or tax year, 30 June, not the calendar year. There are a number of additional processing requirements that must be undertaken annually.

Director loan accounts

If your business is a company or trustee company you must not owe the business any money at the end of the tax year. And you must ensure that all loans are either repaid or converted into salary.

If your business is as a sole trader or partnership, then you are the business and any loan funds are just a matter of balances between your private and business funds. They do not affect your tax liability.

Private use and drawings account

Make sure that the private use / business use of motor vehicles and other assets has been accounted for and any FBT liability satisfied.

Trading stock

As a micro business you do not have to undertake an annual stocktake if you can reasonably estimate that your closing stock levels are within $5000 of your opening stock levels for the year. You should always undertake an annual stocktake for accounting purposes, but you can elect whether or not to use these figures for taxation purposes. If you wish to undertake a stocktake for taxation purposes, you would record the closing stock amounts at this stage.

Small businesses that are over the $2 million turnover limit must undertake an annual stocktake and record the closing stock figures for taxation purposes.

When you undertake an annual stocktake you also undertake an *Impairment Review*, which basically means you look for missing or obsolete stock and adjust your record accordingly. The process of doing an annual stocktake was more fully discussed in chapter 5, on trading stock.

Depreciation

You should account for your depreciation charge on your assets at least annually, although some business owners undertake this quarterly to estimate their profit on a quarter-by-quarter basis. Refer to chapter 4, on capital allowances, for further information.

Annual close-off of the account

Once you are sure that all processing has been completed for the year you can 'close off' the accounts.

For individuals and partnerships, you transfer the net profit figure to a retained earnings account, one for each partner/owner, and then transfer the balance of each partner's drawings account to their respective retained earnings accounts. The drawings accounts now start the new year with a zero balance.

For companies it is a little more complex. By now, all owners' loan accounts should have been satisfied and you should have already converted your owner's drawings accounts into owner's salaries. Both loan and drawings accounts should have a zero balance. You will need to estimate your company's income tax and record this as an Other Expense, to be offset against a liability account, 'Provision for income tax payable'. You now close off the remaining profit to retained earnings.

As a company you will also need to keep a franking account that simply lists your taxable income and tax paid on that income plus details of any dividends paid out of those profits and the amount of tax attached (franked) to those dividends. It's basically a running balance tax account, with tax paid going in and tax distributed as dividends going out.

Annual returns

There are a number of annual returns you may have to fill out:

▶ The FBT return is due within 28 days of 31 March.

▶ The income tax return for the year ending 30 June is due by the end of October (unless late lodgement is approved).

▶ If you elect for an annual GST return, this will be required for the year ending 30 June. The annual statement will be posted to you for completion and is due by the time you lodge your annual income tax return, or 28 February at the latest.

▶ You will also have to fill in an annual payment summary for each of your employees and a reconciliation of the payment summaries and withholding taxes paid on your quarterly BAS.

Annual income tax returns

Individuals in business as sole traders will only need to fill in an individual tax return that includes a business section and pay income tax at personal rates on the calculated taxable income.

Partnerships will fill in a partnership return detailing how much each partner will receive of the net partnership income. Each partner will then fill in their own individual return, including in that their proportion of the partnership income. Each partner will pay income tax at personal rates on the taxable income of their individual tax return.

Companies will fill in their own company's tax return and pay tax at the company tax rate on the taxable profit (assessable income). The directors of the company may decide to pass some or all of this income to the individual shareholders in proportion to their shareholdings (dividends). That tax paid on the income is also passed to the individual shareholder. This process is called a *franked dividend*, and because of the complexities of company accounting, the company annual processing will usually be undertaken by a professional tax accountant.

Companies will also need to fill in a form sent to you by the Australian Securities and Investments Commission on the anniversary of your company's registration date. It is very easy to complete, requiring no more than confirmation of your particulars. You must return the form with an annual company's lodgement fee. The date this form is required is the anniversary of your company's initial incorporation and therefore can occur at any time during the year.

CHAPTER 11
Employing staff

Key areas we will cover in this chapter

▶ Employing staff

▶ What are the components of an employee's wage?

▶ Creating the payslip

▶ Superannuation guarantee

▶ Medicare levy

▶ Employment (eligible) termination payments

Defined terms we will introduce

Ordinary time earnings (OTE): the amount on which superannuation contributions made by an employer on an employee's behalf are based, made up of the employee's 'normal' wage or salary components

Gross income: an amount that includes an employee's OTE but to which is added all other taxable items

Allowances: amounts that make up an employee's wage paid for a specific purpose, such as a dirt or tool allowance. Allowances are treated according to their type: work related or income related.

Work-related expenses: amounts reimbursed through the payroll system to compensate employees for work-related expenditure. They are not included in gross income for withholding tax purposes.

Pay as you go (PAYG): a system by which the amounts of tax you withhold from your employees' wages are transferred to the Tax Office through your quarterly Business Activity Statement (BAS)

Unused leave entitlements: annual and long service leave not used by the employee

Annual leave: an entitlement by full-time and part-time employees to paid leave (usually 20 paid days) each year

Long service leave: leave accrued over a long period, usually three months over 15 years, that is paid out (pro rata) on termination after 10 years

Employment termination payment: amount paid on termination of employment that is not included in the normal last pay and is concessionally taxed, such as a 'golden handshake' (lump sum paid on termination)

Drawings: an amount withdrawn from the business by the owner in cash or goods in anticipation of profits

Salary: fixed annual amount paid to professional and executive staff irrespective of the actual hours worked

Wages: an amount paid to an employee based on an hourly rate

Casual: an employee paid by the hour on a needs basis who may be entitled to overtime if they work more than 38 hours during the week

Contractor: a service provider who works under contract to perform a specific function

Tax offsets: concessional amounts that can be claimed by the taxpayer to offset the normal amount of tax payable

Holiday leave loading: 17.5 per cent of normal pay, paid at the time the employee takes their annual leave; available only to certain employees working under an award that includes this payment.

Medicare levy: 2 per cent included in the tax withheld from salary and wages to pay for the public health system

Superannuation guarantee: an amount based upon a percentage of the employee's OTE that the employer is required to pay into the employee's private superannuation fund

In this chapter we examine the complexities of employing and paying staff. Calculating wages so staff are correctly paid is one of the main areas of concern for small business proprietors, and their concerns are not unfounded. The tax law associated with the correct calculation of taxes withheld from employees' wages is arduous. We explain how to correctly calculate wages and salaries, as well as the necessary recordkeeping requirements.

The legal requirements of employing staff

Before you can employee anyone you must register as an employer with the Tax Office for PAYG withholding tax. Your BAS will then include a field called withholding tax where you include the amount of tax you have withheld from your employees' wages. Irrespective of how often you pay your employees, you only return the amounts withheld to the Tax Office on your monthly or quarterly BAS. Withholding amounts include amounts you withhold from your employees' wages and directors' salaries, as well as amounts withheld from contractors who cannot provide an ABN number.

You should also ensure that you have the correct level of cover of workers compensation insurance (this is a legal requirement) and that your employees have the correct qualifications and accreditations for the work they are to undertake (these requirements are beyond the scope of this text).

Your new employee should fill in a tax file number (TFN) declaration form (see figure 11.1, overleaf). If the employee fails to provide you with the completed form, then you must deduct 49 per cent tax from their net pay. This form provides you with all the information you need to complete a wage or salary calculation, such as:

▶ the employee's TFN

▶ the employee's name and address

▶ whether the employee is an Australian tax resident

▶ whether the employee is claiming the tax-free threshold

▶ whether the employee has a Higher Education Loan Program (HELP) debt, formerly the Higher Education Contribution Scheme (HECS)

▶ whether the employee has a financial supplement debt.

Figure 11.1: tax file number declaration form

ORIGINAL – ATO copy

Australian Government
Australian Taxation Office

ato.gov.au

Tax file number declaration

This declaration is NOT an application for a tax file number.
- Use a black or blue pen and print clearly in BLOCK LETTERS.
- Print X in the appropriate boxes.
- Read all the instructions before you complete this declaration.

30920713

Section A: To be completed by the PAYEE

1 What is your tax file number (TFN)?

For more information, see question 1 on page 2 of the instructions.

OR I have made a separate application/enquiry to the ATO for a new or existing TFN.

OR I am claiming an exemption because I am under 18 years of age and do not earn enough to pay tax.

OR I am claiming an exemption because I am in receipt of a pension, benefit or allowance.

2 What is your name? Title: Mr Mrs Miss Ms

Surname or family name

First given name

Other given names

3 If you have changed your name since you last dealt with us, show your previous family name

4 What is your date of birth? Day Month Year

5 What is your home address in Australia?

Suburb or town

State/territory Postcode

6 On what basis are you paid? (Select only one.)
Full-time employment / Part-time employment / Labour hire / Superannuation or annuity income stream / Casual employment

7 Are you an Australian resident for tax purposes? Yes No — You must answer no at question 8.
(Visit ato.gov.au/residency to check)

8 Do you want to claim the tax-free threshold from this payer?
Only claim the tax-free threshold from one payer at a time, unless your total income from all sources for the financial year will be less than the tax-free threshold.
Yes No — Answer no at questions 9 and 10 unless you are a foreign resident claiming a seniors and pensioners, zone or overseas forces tax offset.

9 Do you want to claim the seniors and pensioners tax offset by reducing the amount withheld from payments made to you?
Yes — Complete a *Withholding declaration* (NAT 3093), but only if you are claiming the tax-free threshold from this payer. If you have more than one payer, see page 3 of the instructions. No

10 Do you want to claim a zone, overseas forces, dependent spouse or dependent (invalid and carer) tax offset by reducing the amount withheld from payments made to you?
Yes — Complete a *Withholding declaration* (NAT 3093) No

11 (a) Do you have an accumulated Higher Education Loan Program (HELP) debt?
Yes — Your payer will withhold additional amounts to cover any compulsory repayments that may be raised on your notice of assessment. No

(b) Do you have an accumulated Financial Supplement debt?
Yes — Your payer will withhold additional amounts to cover any compulsory repayments that may be raised on your notice of assessment. No

DECLARATION by payee: *I declare that the information I have given is true and correct.*

Signature — You MUST SIGN here — Date Day Month Year

There are penalties for deliberately making a false or misleading statement.

Sample only

Once section A is completed and signed, give it to your payer to complete section B.

Section B: To be completed by the PAYER (if you are not lodging online)

1 What is your Australian business number (ABN) or your withholding payer number? Branch number (if applicable)

2 If you don't have an ABN or withholding payer number, have you applied for one? Yes No

3 What is your legal name or registered business name (or your individual name if not in business)?

DECLARATION by payer: *I declare that the information I have given is true and correct.*

Signature of payer — Date Day Month Year

There are penalties for deliberately making a false or misleading statement.

4 What is your business address?

Suburb or town

State/territory Postcode

5 Who is your contact person?

Business phone number

6 If you no longer make payments to this payee, print X in this box

Return the completed original ATO copy to:
For WA, SA, NT, VIC or TAS: Australian Taxation Office, PO Box 795, ALBURY NSW 2640
For NSW, QLD or ACT: Australian Taxation Office, PO Box 9004, PENRITH NSW 2740

IMPORTANT
See reverse side of Payer's copy for:
- payer obligations
- lodging online.

TAXPAYER-SENSITIVE (when completed)

NAT 3092-07.2013 [JS 27654]

You complete your details, such as ABN and company name, on the second part of the form. Send the original form to the Tax Office within 14 days and keep a copy on the employee's file. You must also provide the employee's superannuation fund with the employee's TFN number.

Tax residency

Australians' liability to tax is based on the concept of tax *residency*, not citizenship. Australian tax residents are generally taxed on their worldwide income, whereas non-residents are generally taxed only on their Australian-sourced income.

You are considered to be an Australian resident for tax purposes if you:

▶ have always lived in Australia or you have come to Australia to live

▶ have been in Australia for more than half of the income year (unless your usual home is overseas and you do not intend to live in Australia; for example, if you are a working holiday maker)

▶ are an overseas student enrolled in a course of study for more than six months.

The tax rates that apply depend on whether or not you are an Australian resident. A higher rate of tax is applied to a non-resident's Australian income and non-residents are not entitled to a tax-free threshold. Non-residents also have limited access to Medicare and social security. Lower tax rates and the tax-free threshold apply to Australian tax residents, but they pay that tax on their worldwide income.

Tax-free threshold

Only Australian tax residents can claim the tax-free threshold of the first $18 200 of their income. Employees can claim the tax-free threshold from only one employer each year, so if you are employing someone such as a casual and this is their second job, they may not be able to claim the tax-free threshold.

Higher Education Loan Program (HELP)

A HELP debt is money that the taxpayer borrowed from the federal government to subsidise their education. The debt is repaid through the tax system once the taxpayer income reaches a certain level ($53 345 per annum for 2015 and reducing to $46 179 per annum in 2016). The tax applied starts at a rate of 4 per cent and rises as the income level increases to 8 per cent once your employee's annual income reaches $99 070.

Financial supplement debt

This student loan scheme closed in 2003; however, some of your employees may still have an outstanding debt.

Employee requests

Employees may also require that you take into account a rebate to which they are entitled or to vary the tax rate that applies when calculating their tax. Such requests must be made in writing. If the employee wants to pay less tax, their request must be made through a Tax Office variation authorisation.

All of the processes mentioned so far can be completed using computer-based applications. If you have fewer than 10 employees you can make the calculations manually using a tax calculator that can be downloaded from the ATO site. For more than 10 but fewer than 20 employees, I strongly suggest you use a payroll package such as MYOB. For more than 20 employees a payroll service is the way to go.

Wages and salaries

Wages are traditionally calculated on an hourly basis while a salary is a fixed amount per month or year. Casual rates are paid per hour of attendance and are usually higher than the rates paid to permanent employees. Some employees are paid by commission, or a base salary plus commission. Bonuses are often part of the salary package and in some instances may be an unexpected reward for good service.

Ordinary time earnings (OTE)

Our first priority is to work out our employee's base wage or ordinary time earnings (OTE). OTE include employees' earnings for ordinary hours of work as well as over-award payments, paid leave, commissions and shift allowances.

Our first step is to calculate the two types of income, the OTE and the larger amount of gross income for tax purposes. Both of these amounts include an employee's base wage, but it is on the question of penalties and allowances that the differences apply.

Penalties and allowances

It is not unusual for an employee's entitlements to include amounts that are in addition to their base rate of pay. For instance, shift workers receive a penalty payment as compensation for working outside normal business hours and tradespeople often get a tool allowance for using their own tools on the job. Some allowances are not subject to tax and are not included in the wage calculations at all, such as reimbursement for business-related expenditure. Some allowances are included in both OTE and gross income, while others are included only in gross income.

Payments included in OTE and gross income include:

▶ 'normal' wages or salary for hours worked

▶ allowances for qualifications, such as first aid or safety qualifications

▶ allowances that are not reimbursement of expenses

▶ meals that are not part of the employment award, as well as danger, dirt, height, shift and travelling time allowances

▶ bonuses related to specific performance

▶ commissions

▶ over-award payments

▶ shift loading

▶ casual loading

▶ annual holiday leave taken

▶ sick leave taken

▶ long service leave

▶ government subsidies such as Job Start.

In addition to the payments listed above, the following payments are included in gross income:

▶ overtime

▶ allowances for tax-deductible items

▶ uniform laundry of more than $150 per year, uniform dry cleaning, tools, motor vehicle paid over the tax rate or for non-deductible (private) use

- bonuses not related to specific performance, such as a Christmas bonus

- jury duty or reserve forces top-up payments

- maternity or paternity leave

- annual leave loading

- accrued leave paid on termination

- redundancy or payments in lieu of notice

- other payments paid on termination, such as severance pay.

Payments outside the wages tax calculation that are shown on the payslip and payment summary include:

- reimbursement for deductible business-related expenses, such as motor vehicle reimbursement within Tax Office guidelines, tool allowances and other work-related expenses

- an expense allowance paid in expectation that it will be fully expended for business-related purposes (any private use or retained surplus is taxable)

- workers' compensation payments including salary top-ups

- benefits paid that are subject to fringe benefits tax.

Payments outside the wages calculation that are shown on the payslip but not on the payment summary include:

- reasonable domestic travel costs

- reasonable amounts for meal allowances paid under an award.

Reasonable amounts for domestic travel and award meal allowances are published on the Tax Office website (see tax determination TD 2013/16).

Allowances

Employees may be paid a variety of allowances. *Work-related expenses outside of wages tax calculation* refers to the payment of an allowance for which the employee can claim a compensating deduction on their tax return. Therefore, as an employer you do not tax this allowance, but it must be declared on the employee's tax return and an offsetting deduction claimed. Any difference is taxable to the employee.

Annual leave loading is an additional 17.5 per cent loading (to a maximum of $320) paid to workers taking annual leave provided that such a leave loading arrangement is part of that worker's industrial award—for example, cleaners. You must pay the 17.5 per cent annual leave loading calculated on the employee's ordinary time rate of pay, which is not the same as the ordinary times earnings for superannuation purposes but is an amount defined separately in each award. Employees entitled to a leave loading pay a slightly higher rate of tax throughout the year so that the amount of the loading is not taxed when it is taken.

If you are unsure of which award your workers fall under, contact the Department of Commerce for guidance.

Annual leave is paid time off that an employee usually uses for recreational purposes, such as to take a holiday. Full-time employees are entitled to four weeks of paid annual leave for every year they work for your business. Part-time employees receive a pro rata amount of annual leave, which means a proportionate amount based on their hours of work. Casual employees are not paid annual leave. If your business employs shift workers, they may be entitled to an additional week of annual leave every year. You and your employees need to agree on a time for them to take annual leave and you cannot 'unreasonably refuse' the request.

When an employee finishes working for your business, all of their unused annual leave must be paid out to them at the amount they would have received if they had taken the annual leave, including any leave loading.

Workers' compensation payments are outside the wages system only where there is no work involved on behalf of the employee in order to receive the payment. If the payment requires some form of work commitment, then it is included in both OTE and gross income as a normal wage or salary.

Superannuation (superannuation guarantee)

Employees aged between 18 and 69 years who earn more than $450 per month must have 9.5 per cent (rising to 12 per cent by July 2019) of OTE paid into a complying superannuation fund (or retirement savings account) of their choice. It makes no difference whether the employee is employed full time or part time, or on a contract or casual basis, the employer must still contribute 9.5 per cent of their OTE to a superannuation fund. If your employee is younger than 18 years of age and works more than 30 hours per week, they are also eligible for a 9.5 per cent superannuation contribution. The payments start from your employee's first pay. A maximum salary tops the payment, and for 2015 that is $49 430 per quarter or $197 720 per year.

The payment must be made within 28 days after the end of each quarter for all salary and wage payments in that quarter. The payment of your employee's superannuation contribution is deductible to the business, but only when it has been paid, not when it was accrued.

If you fail to provide these superannuation payments for your employees you will receive a penalty, the superannuation guarantee charge. The penalty is based on the amount that should have been paid, an interest charge of 10 per cent plus an administration charge. The superannuation guarantee charge is a penalty so it is not tax deductible.

Putting it all together

Here are some examples that apply what you've learned so far in this chapter.

Example 1: determining Alex's OTE and gross earnings

You employ a tradesperson as a wages employee at $35 per hour. Alex provides her own van and tools, and claims an allowance for the use of these. Overtime is in addition to normal wages.

For the pay fortnight Alex works 9 eight-hour days and has one eight-hour day of sick leave. She works one Saturday morning for four hours overtime at time and a half. Her tool allowance is $50 per week and mileage is paid at the tax rate of 60c per kilometre of work-related travel. She travelled 375 kilometres in the fortnight and has submitted a mileage claim for the period.

What are her OTE, gross income for tax purposes and additional work-related payments?

Answer

OTE includes normal hours wages and sick leave:

Hours worked:	9 days × 8 hours @ $35	2520.00
Sick leave:	8 hours @ $35	280.00
		2800.00

Additional amounts included in gross income:

Overtime:	4 hours @ 1.5 at $35	210.00
		3010.00

Non-taxable business-related expenditure reimbursement:

Mileage allowance 350 km at $0.60	210.00
Tool allowance: 2 weeks at $50	100.00
	3320.00

Superannuation is paid at 9.5 per cent of OTE and tax calculated on the total gross earnings. Non-taxable business-related expenses are not taxed as part of the PAYG system, but are included in the employee's own tax return along with an offsetting claim for a deduction for business-related expenditure.

Doing the calculations

Now we have both OTE and gross earnings we can do the necessary calculations.

Superannuation contribution

The superannuation contribution is 9.5 per cent of OTE:

$$9.5\% \times \$2800 = \$266$$

The superannuation amount is shown on the payslip but is not included in any of the amounts payable. Each employee could have their own salary account and associated superannuation account as above so you can track the individual payments as needed. Alternatively you could keep the details separate in each employee's pay file, in which case the debit entry would be to a general salary and wage on-cost account rather than the individual's superannuation account.

Every quarter you pay out the superannuation amount to the individual employee's superannuation fund. To facilitate this, set up a spreadsheet file with the employee's name, superannuation fund and employee superannuation number. Some funds allow you to pay into their account electronically, while others require a cheque and an accompanying schedule of contributions. A retirement savings account (RSA) that employees can open with some banks to hold small amounts of superannuation payments may even require you to complete something similar to a bank deposit slip.

If you are a small business with fewer than 20 employees, you can use the facility set up by the Australian government and administered by Medicare called the small business superannuation clearing house. This facility allows you to pay one bulk amount into an account with Medicare and have Medicare make the individual distributions for you. More information on this service can be found at www.medicareaustralia.gov.au/super.

PAYG income tax

PAYG income tax is the crux of the whole payroll system. You can use six separate schedules to work out the amount of tax to be deducted from an employee's wage, including income tax, Medicare levy and HECS (Student Loan) type repayments. Each of these schedules is available for weekly, fortnightly or monthly wage calculations. There are 18 separate schedules, each of which varies from year to year, so which one do you use?

There are three basic ways you calculate the tax that you must withhold. You can do this manually, using a payroll package such as MYOB or using a payroll service. Fortunately the Tax Office makes the manual calculation a lot easier than using the traditional paper-based approach. If you go to the Tax Office site at www.ato.gov.au and type TWC into the search field it will bring up details for a tax withheld calculation application that you can use for this purpose.

Employee deductions

Generally speaking, an employer is allowed to make a deduction from an employee's pay if:

▶ the employee agreed in writing and the deduction is principally for the employee's benefit

▶ the employee authorised the deduction in accordance with an enterprise agreement

▶ the deduction is authorised by or under an award or an order of Fair Work Australia

▶ the deduction is authorised by or under a law or an order of a court.

However, an employer cannot make a deduction from an employee's pay even if it is authorised by an award or an enterprise agreement if the:

▶ deduction is for the benefit of the employer or is partly related to the employer and is unreasonable in the circumstances

▶ employee is under 18 years of age and the employee's guardian or parent hasn't authorised the deduction in writing.

There are two types of deductions:

▶ those that 'come off the top'—that is, they are not included in your employee's wage or salary and are usually referred to as salary sacrifice amounts

▶ those that you make from the after-tax net income amount.

You can legally deduct amounts from an employee's wage only where you hold that request from the employee in writing or it is covered as part of an award agreement. Employers cannot make ad-hoc deductions from an employee's legal entitlement.

Salary sacrifice

There are three types of salary sacrifice.

The first is an amount of additional superannuation that the employee requests (in writing) be deducted each pay and sent, along with the usual 9.5 per cent employer contribution, to the employee's superannuation fund. Although legally this deducted amount does not have to be included in the OTE for the purposes of calculating the 9.5 per cent employer's contribution, it is normal business practice to do so. Superannuation can be deducted from an employee's wage before tax without incurring any fringe benefits tax (FBT) liability.

The second common type of pre-tax deduction is where an employee 'purchases' additional leave. This is in fact a leave-without-pay arrangement where wages are adjusted over time to account for the additional leave period. There are no tax implications in making such an arrangement and whether the amount is included in the employee's OTE is a matter of negotiation at the time that the employee applies to go onto the scheme.

The third but far less common deduction is where an employee requests that amounts of pre-tax wages be applied for their private use. This automatically triggers an FBT problem and therefore is not usually accepted by the employer, except in a few very specific circumstances. This was discussed in more depth in chapter 7, on FBT.

The payslip

Calculating gross income and OTE is a different process from that used to create the payslip. Every employee is entitled to receive a payslip, even if they are on leave, within one working day of the pay date. The payslip can be in hard copy form or electronic, provided that the employee has access to, and can print a copy of, the electronic form. An increasing number of employers are using a PDF attachment to an email for this purpose.

The employee's payslip must include:

▶ the name of the employer (for example, XYZ Pty Ltd trading as XYZ Pie Shop)

▶ the Australian business number (ABN) of the employer

▶ the employee's name

▶ the date of payment

▶ the pay period (for example, 16/3/15 to 29/3/15)

▶ the gross and net amount of pay

▶ any loadings, monetary allowances, bonuses, incentive-based payments, penalty rates or other entitlements paid that can be singled out

▶ if the employee is paid an hourly rate, the ordinary hourly pay rate and number of hours worked at that rate and the amount of pay at that rate

▶ if the employee is paid an annual rate (salary), the rate as at the last day in the pay period

▶ any deductions made from your employee's pay, including the amount and details of each deduction (including superannuation) as well as the name, or the name and number, of the fund or account the deductions are paid into (see figure 11.2)

▶ if you are required to pay superannuation contributions for your employee's benefit:

– the amount of each superannuation contribution made during the period to which the payslip relates, or the amounts of contributions that you are liable to make

– the name or the name and number of the superannuation fund you put or will put superannuation contributions into.

Figure 11.2: pay deductions request

Alex requires us to pay her union dues of $35 per fortnight and her Medibank Private health cover of $55 per week. She also requests that we deduct an extra $50 in income tax. All requests have been made in writing.

Figure 11.3 (overleaf) is an example of a complete payslip. A sample payslip in Excel is available from my website at www.tpabusiness.com.au.

Figure 11.3: a complete payslip

Big Daddy Electrical Contractors

22 Fairfield Crescent, Nowhere NSW 2789
ABN 1234 12345

Pay date	31/3/15	
Employee	Ms Alex Hanson	
Pay period	16/3/2015 to 29/3/2015	

Wages

Wages	9 days at 8 hours at $35.00	2520.00
Overtime	4 hours at 1.5	210.00
Sick leave	8 hours	280.00
		3010.00

Allowances

Tool allowance		100.00
Mileage	350 km at $0.60	210.00
Gross pay		**3320.00**

Deductions

Income tax		715.00
Additional tax		50.00
Union dues	(Electrical Trades Union)	35.00
Medibank Private		55.00
Amount paid	**(ANZ ***345)**	**2465.00**

Leave details

Leave type	Annual entitlement	Opening balance (hrs)	Accrued (hrs)	Used (hrs)	Closing balance (hrs)
Annual leave	20 days	66.5	6.4	0	70.9
Sick leave	10 days	25.2	3.2	8	20.4

Superannuation
9.5 per cent employer's contribution of $266.00 paid into ETU Superannuation.

When you employ people under a modern award or agreement you are legally required to keep accurate and complete time and wages records and issue payslips to each employee. You must keep all time and wages records of each employee for at least seven years. These records should be in plain English and easy to read.

Employees are entitled to know the exact balance of their leave at all times. You must keep accurate and current records of all leave balances. The easiest way to do this in a small business with fewer than 10 employees is to keep a spreadsheet for each employee with their full details that you can cut and paste into a word processing document each payday.

Annual reporting requirements

It is a legal requirement that you provide each employee with a payment summary (what used to be known as a group certificate) within 28 days of the end of the financial year. This payment summary contains details of all payments you have made to the employee for the purpose of allowing the employee to complete their annual tax return.

However, the payment summary, a copy of which you forward to the Tax Office, is also used by the Tax Office to calculate other employee obligations such as child support. For this reason, it also contains information on payments made on the employee's behalf such as salary sacrifice amounts and employer payments that are subject to fringe benefits tax (referred to as reportable fringe benefit amounts).

PAYG payment summary forms and a set of instructions are available from the Tax Office (see figure 11.4, overleaf). The form is a three-part pre-carbonised form—the original is sent to the Tax Office, the second copy is for your employee and has employee instructions printed on the reverse, and the third copy is for your records, to be filed in the employee's pay file.

Figure 11.4: PAYG payment summary

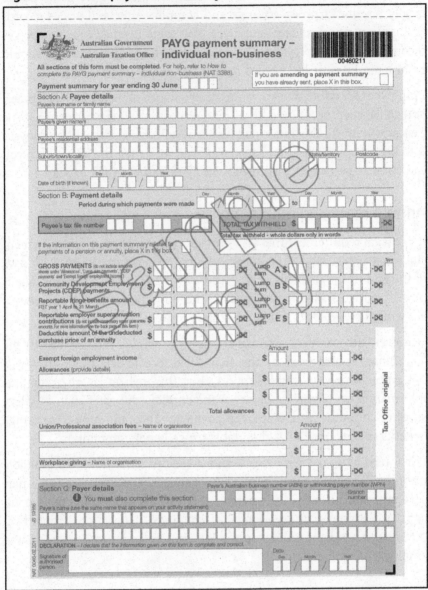

The payment summary is in three sections. Section A shows employee details such as name, address and date of birth, which are required for identification purposes. Section B contains payment details that we discuss below, and section C is for the employer's name, ABN and signature to the declaration.

Section B, payment details, is where you enter the payroll information. Note that the amounts are entered in whole dollars only—ignore the cents.

You need to include the following information in section B:

▶ payment period—usually 1/7/Y1 to 30/6/Y2

▶ employee's TFN—as per the employee's TFN declaration

▶ total tax withheld—in dollars and words

▶ gross payments—includes the gross amount of all payments such as wages, salary, overtime, bonuses and commissions, as well as any outstanding leave balances paid on resignation

▶ reportable fringe benefits—certain FBT items of more than $2000 in total

▶ reportable employer superannuation—include any superannuation payments made over and above the 9.5 per cent superannuation contribution, such as salary sacrifice amounts

▶ allowances paid—for work-related expenses *not* included in the gross income amount, such as tool allowance and motor vehicle allowance. The payments must be shown in detail. If there is not enough room, report as 'various' and attach a detailed breakdown for each payment made.

▶ union/professional fees—the name and payment made to the association. This amount should be included in the gross income amount.

CDEP and annuity payments are included in section B but are beyond the realm of a normal small business employer–employee relationship.

Example 2: Alex's annual payment summary

If Alex had been employed for 20 weeks during the year, what would her annual payment summary contain?

PAYG payment summary

Section A	Payee details		
	Payee surname	Hanson	
	Payee given name	Alex	
	Payee address	123 Anywhere Street	
		Nowhere NSW 3456	
	Date of birth	20/11/1985	

Section B	Payment details		
	Period	01/07/2014 to 30/06/2015	
	Payee TFN	345678912	
	Total tax withheld	15 300 fifteen thousand three hundred dollars	
	Gross payments	60 200	
	Allowances	Tools	2000
		Mileage	4200
	Union dues	Electrical Trades Union	700

Section C	Payer details		
	Payer's ABN	1234 12345	
	Payer's name	Big Daddy Electrical Contractors	

Note that the layout of the payslip matches the information required on the payment summary. The closer the payslip matches the requirements of the payment summary, the easier it is for you to complete the payment summary.

Paying the boss — drawings versus salary

It is normal for a business owner to take an amount of cash or goods out of the business on a regular basis. This drawing is more than likely referred to as the owner's wages.

However, if you run your own small business, either as a sole proprietor (such as a lawn mowing contractor) or in a partnership, then you cannot 'legally' pay yourself a salary or wage. Any monies (or goods) that you take out of the business are considered a drawing in anticipation of profits (a reduction in equity) and not a salary or wage expense. No taxes are withheld from the owner's drawings. The owner's income tax liability is based on the profits of the business.

On the other hand, if you are the owner of a company (a director in the legal sense), your drawings are classed as a salary or wage and you will need to be 'employed'; that is, abide by the same legal and tax requirements as any other employee. In the case of a company, the entity pays company tax and the owner pays income tax on their salary (drawings), and includes the company dividends and franking credits in their annual tax returns.

Employee or contractor?

The first question we must ask ourselves is, 'who exactly are our employees?'

Businesses often employ staff who are employees under the common law definition of master and servant, but they can also employ staff under contractual arrangements. If these staff are employed through an agency with whom you have an ongoing relationship—that is, the agency bills you for the employee's time and you settle the account with the agency—then the employee is a contractor and therefore outside the PAYG system (as far as your business is concerned). However, if contractors are employed directly by the business, at what point does a contract employee become a wages employee?

A number of factors need to be considered in determining whether a worker is an employee or an independent contractor, with no one factor necessarily being conclusive. A key factor in deciding if a worker is an employee is the *degree of control* that can be exercised over the worker. If the employer has the right to direct how, when, where and who is to perform the work, the worker is likely to be an employee. These directions may be verbal or in writing, or simply understood between the parties.

Another key factor to consider is whether the worker is being paid for the *time* they work, or being paid for a *result*. Workers being paid by the hour are more likely to be employees. Workers being paid for a result are more likely to be independent contractors.

Generally a worker is an employee if they:

▶ are paid for time worked

▶ receive paid leave (for example, sick, annual or recreation, or long service leave)

▶ are not responsible for providing the materials or equipment required to do their job

▶ must perform the duties of their position

▶ agree to provide their personal services

▶ work hours set by an agreement or award

▶ are recognised as part and parcel of the payer's business

▶ take no commercial risks and cannot make a profit or loss from the work performed.

An independent contractor is an entity (such as an individual, partnership, trust or company) that agrees to produce a designated result for an agreed price. In most cases an independent contractor:

▶ is paid for results achieved

▶ provides all or most of the necessary materials and equipment to complete the work

▶ is free to delegate work to other entities

▶ has freedom in the way the work is done

▶ provides services to the general public and other businesses

▶ is free to accept or refuse work

▶ is in a position to make a profit or loss.

An employee is paid a wage and has tax and other deductions taken from their pay, whereas a contractor provides you with an invoice that includes a bill for their services and GST where applicable. You pay this invoice as you would any other expense.

Contractors are not usually covered by your workers compensation and therefore you should ensure that all workers have their own workers compensation insurance coverage.

Tax offsets

Item 10 on your employee's tax file number (employee) declaration asks if the employee wants to claim zone, overseas forces, dependant spouse or special tax offsets. What are these?

Tax offsets can be claimed by a taxpayer in certain circumstances through their annual tax return. Examples include a zone allowance, where the employee works in a remote location, or a spouse rebate, where the employee's spouse's income is less than a prescribed amount. These amounts are claimed by the employee through a withholding declaration form. The amount claimed on this form is a matter between the employee and the Tax Office. If you receive the form then you include the payday amount in your payroll calculations for that employee.

The withholding declaration form is also used to vary any information originally provided on the tax file number (employee) declaration form and also is used where the employee wishes to vary the amount of tax you withhold from their wages.

Holiday leave loading

Certain industrial award conditions, such as the award for cleaners, require that an employer pay the employee 17.5 per cent of their normal wages as a loading when the employee takes annual leave. For example, if an employee's normal pay is $2000 per fortnight and they go on leave for the fortnight, then you are required to pay them an additional $350 in leave loading. The main problem with leave loading is that it is taxed progressively throughout the year and not at the time of payment. Because of this, when you pay leave loading at the time the employee takes their leave, it is included in the holiday payslip as a non-taxed amount.

Medicare levy variation

Some employees earning less than prescribed amounts who have a certain number of child dependants can claim an exemption from the Medicare levy. They do this on a form supplied by the Tax Office (see figure 11.5, overleaf). If an employee provides you with this form then again you must include this when calculating the payroll for this employee.

Figure 11.5: Medicare levy variation declaration form

Australian Government
Australian Taxation Office

Medicare levy variation declaration form

- Refer to the Instructions to help you complete this declaration.
- Print neatly in BLOCK LETTERS and use a black or dark blue pen.
- Print ☒ in the appropriate boxes.

❶ The information in the completed *Medicare levy variation declaration* form must be treated as sensitive.

Section A: Payee's declaration

➤ To be completed by payee.

1 **What is your tax file number (TFN)?**

➤ See 'Privacy' on the inside front cover of the Instructions.

2 **What is your name?**

Title: Mr ☐ Mrs ☐ Miss ☐ Ms ☐ Other

Family name

Given names

3 **What is your home address?**

Street address

Suburb/town   State/Territory   Postcode

4 **Do you want your payer to increase the amounts withheld from you to cover the Medicare levy surcharge?**
No ☐ Go to question 5.   Yes ☐ Select one of the following rates

1% ☐   1.25% ☐   1.5% ☐

If you want to make other variations using this form, go to question 5. Otherwise, sign and date the declaration and give it to your payer.

5 **Do you qualify for a Medicare levy exemption?**
No ☐ Go to question 9.   Yes ☐

6 **Do you want to claim a full exemption from the Medicare levy?**
No ☐   Yes ☐ Go to question 9.

7 **Do you want to claim a half exemption from the Medicare levy?**
No ☐   Yes ☐ Go to question 9.

8 **Do you want to claim a Medicare levy reduction?**
No ☐   Yes ☐

9 **Do you have a spouse?**
No ☐   Yes ☐
➤ For a definition of spouse, see Definitions on page 5.

10 **Is the combined weekly income of you and your spouse, or your income as a sole parent, less than the relevant amount in table A on page 1?**
No ☐   Yes ☐

11a **Do you have an accumulated Higher Education Loan Program (HELP) debt?**
No ☐   Yes ☐ If you also answered yes at question 10, you are exempt from having additional PAYG amounts for HELP withheld from payments to you.

11b **Do you have an accumulated Financial Supplement debt?**
No ☐   Yes ☐ If you also answered yes at question 10, you are exempt from having additional PAYG amounts for Financial Supplement debts withheld from payments to you.

12 **Do you have dependent children?**
No ☐ Sign and date the declaration.   Yes ☐ How many?

➤ For a definition of dependent children, see Definitions on page 5.

NAT 0929-07.2013   **Sensitive** (when completed)

Termination of employment

In this discussion we limit ourselves to the normal 'brown bag' termination where an employee leaves of their own accord. We do not discuss redundancy, retirement or forced resignation. We also assume that your employee has been with your firm for less than 15 years.

When an employee terminates their employment, they are paid out any leave balance owing. Leave balances, including annual leave and any long service leave (including pro rata payments) are included in an employee's gross income and taxed accordingly. There are no longer any special tax provisions for these types of payments.

Example 3: Alex's last day

The payday of 14/06/2015 was Alex's last day with the firm. How would this modify the payslip and the income summary?

Her annual leave entitlement of 70.9 hours must be paid out and added to her gross income. Her sick leave entitlement is forgone and she has no accrued long service leave:

$$70.9 \times \$35.00 = \$2481.50$$

Taxation of unused leave entitlements on termination

You cannot just add the unused leave payments to gross income because the tax calculated would be excessive. Taxation rules require that such calculations use only the normal marginal rate of tax that is applied to normal gross income tax calculations. 'Marginal' means the tax as a percentage of the last dollar added to gross income.

Use the following calculation to calculate the correct amount of tax:

1   Calculate the tax in the normal way but only on the 'normal' gross income without the unused leave balances included. This is $715.

2   Calculate the amount of unused leave payments, in our case $2481.50, and divide that by the number of pay periods in the year, in our case 26:

$2481.50 \div 26 = \$95.44$

3   To the normal gross income add 1/26th of the leave payment:

3010.00 + 95.44 = $3105.44

4   Calculate the tax on this figure. This comes to $749.

5   Work out the difference between the two tax amounts:

$749 − $715 = $34

then multiply that difference by 26:

$34 × $26 = $884.

So $884 is the tax payable on the unused leave balance paid on termination of employment.

Total tax payable is:

$715 + $884 = $1599.

The termination payslip is shown in figure 11.6.

Figure 11.6: termination payslip

Big Daddy Electrical Contractors		
22 Fairfield Crescent, Nowhere NSW 2789		
ABN 1234 12345		
Pay date	19/06/2015	*Termination pay*
Employee	Ms Alex Hanson	
Pay period	01/06/2015 to 14/06/2015	
Wages		
Wages	9 days at 8 hours at $35.00	2520.00
Overtime	4 hours at 1.5	210.00
Sick leave	8 hours	280.00
	Normal pay for this period	3010.00
Annual leave	70.9 hours @ $35.00	2481.50
		5491.50
Allowances		
Tool allowance		100.00
Mileage	230k at $0.60	210.00
Gross pay		**5801.50**

Deductions

Income tax on normal pay		715.00
Income tax payable on leave balances		884.00
Additional tax		50.00
Union dues	(Electrical Trades Union)	35.00
Medibank Private		55.00
Amount paid	**(ANZ ***345)**	**4062.50**

Superannuation

9.5 per cent employer's contribution of $266.00 paid into ETU Superannuation.

Employment termination payments

An employment (formerly eligible) termination payment (ETP), paid on the termination of an employee's employment, is the payment of certain amounts that are concessionally taxed, depending on the type and age of the payment. Significant changes were made in the taxation of ETPs in July 2007 (although some transitional changes apply until June 2012):

▶ ETPs can no longer be rolled over into superannuation (except transitional arrangements).

▶ ETPs need to be made within 12 months of termination to qualify for reduced tax benefits (excluding genuine redundancy payments).

▶ A cap or limit applies for amounts to qualify for the lower tax benefit.

Payments in ETPs include:

▶ payment in lieu of notice

▶ payout of rostered days off entitlement

▶ a gratuity, golden handshake or compensation for loss of employment

▶ payments resulting in termination because of ill health, invalidity or personal injury

▶ payments for wrongful dismissal

▶ payments for genuine redundancy or early retirement in excess of tax-free limit.

Amounts that accumulated for pre-1983 employment or as a consequence of invalidity may be tax free in some circumstances. The transitional arrangements that apply to the taxation of ETPs apply only to amounts paid under a contract that was in force as at 9 May 2006. Special arrangements apply to death benefits paid as an ETP.

A detailed discussion of these provisions is beyond the 'brown bag' scope of this text. Please refer to the Tax Office publication on employment termination payments for further information in these cases.

The taxation of ETPs

How ETPs are taxed depends on the ETP cap. The ETP cap amount for the 2014–15 financial year is $185 000. The ETP cap is indexed in line with the average weekly ordinary time earnings (AWOTE) in increments of $5000 (rounded down).

▶ If the total amount of the payment (even if paid in a number of instalments over different tax years) exceeds the cap, then the excess is taxed at 49 per cent.

▶ If the total payments do not exceed the cap amount and the employee is less than their preservation age on the last day of the income year, then a flat tax rate of 32 per cent applies.

▶ If the total payments do not exceed the cap amount and the employee is more than their preservation age, then a flat tax rate of 17 per cent applies.

The preservation age for individuals born before 1 July 1960 is 55 years of age. For individuals born after this date, it is the age you can retire and access your super.

If you need to make an ETP payment, report it to the Tax Office on a PAYG payment summary—employment termination payment form (see figure 11.7).

Figure 11.7: PAYG payment summary—employment termination payment form

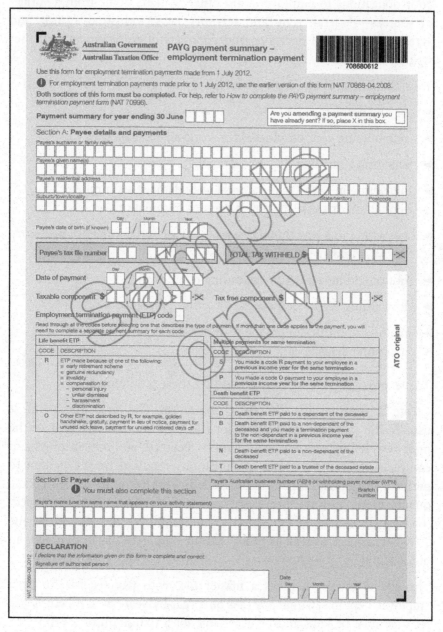

Keeping records

Your obligations to employees and other workers come from a variety of sources—federal, state and territory laws, industrial awards and agreements, tribunal decisions and contracts of employment (whether written or verbal).

Your obligations as an employer include:

▶ paying correct wages

▶ reimbursing your employees for work-related expenses

▶ ensuring a safe working environment

▶ not acting in a way that may seriously damage an employee's reputation or cause mental distress or humiliation

▶ not acting in a way that damages the trust and confidence necessary for an employment relationship

▶ not providing a false or misleading reference

▶ forwarding PAYE tax instalments to the Tax Office

▶ making appropriate payment under the superannuation guarantee legislation.

The records you keep help you to satisfy these requirements.

Create a separate file for each employee. The first document is usually the person's application for the position, records kept of the interview, letters sent and acceptances received, and any employment contracts entered into. The qualifications required by the person to perform the job should also be included—for example, proof of trade qualifications and any necessary trade certification. Once employed, the first document to be added to the employee file should be the TFN declaration, as well as proof that the employee has undertaken an indoctrination procedure.

This file is usually kept as a master file, with pay records for each employee kept in separate pay files on a year-by-year basis. All employee records must be kept and be accessible for a minimum of seven years, and are private and confidential. Generally no-one can access the records other than the employee, employer and relevant payroll staff.

Your records, when viewed as a whole, must at least show the following:

► the name of the employer and the name of the employee

► the Australian Business Number (ABN) (if any) of the employer

► the date the employee started employment

► whether the employee is full time or part time

► whether the employee is permanent, temporary or casual

► the employee's pay rate, including gross and net amounts paid and any deductions from the gross amount

► any loadings, monetary allowances, bonuses, incentive-based payments, penalty rates or other entitlements paid that can be singled out

► whether a penalty rate or loading must be paid for overtime hours actually worked, the number of hours of overtime worked, or when the employee started and finished working overtime

► hours worked if the employee works casual or irregular part-time hours and is guaranteed a pay rate set by reference to a period of time worked

► a copy of the written agreement if you and your employee have agreed to average the employee's work hours.

► whether you and your employee have agreed to an individual flexibility arrangement, a copy of that agreement and, if the agreement is terminated, a copy of the termination

► leave information for all types of leave, including:

  – leave taken

  – leave balance

  – a copy of any agreement to cash out accrued leave, the rate of payment for the leave and when the payment was made

► for employees paid superannuation (excluding payments to a defined benefit fund), the:

  – amount paid

  – pay period

  – date(s) paid

- name of super fund
- reason you paid super into the fund (for example, a record of the employee's super fund choice and the date that choice was made)

▶ if the employment is terminated:

- who terminated the employment
- how the termination took place — by consent, notice, summarily or in some other way (include details).

Payroll fraud

Some employees will be tempted to steal from their employer.

There is a simple rule that will help you prevent employees stealing from you and that is to be vigilant. If you do not double-check, or have checks and balances in place, then you will be targeted. A disgruntled employee, an employee under financial strain or an employee with a gambling or drug habit are all potential instigators of fraud. No-one is immune. Payroll fraud can happen at any time and in a variety of ways. We deal with two of the most common types of payroll fraud: phantom employees and payroll manipulation.

Phantom employees

A phantom employee is an employee who exists only on paper within your payroll system, not in reality. The head count of your employees is one of the most basic auditing techniques, used both by your own internal or external audit staff and also by the Tax Office, union and WorkCover payroll auditors.

Phantom employees can be created in a variety of ways. The most common is where a line manager has the ability to hire staff and there are no counterchecks on this. For example, a warehouse manager may be able to employ casual staff and needs only to send through the TFN declaration and employee details as proof of employment for payroll purposes. In this situation, it is too easy for the manager to submit fake details of a short-term casual employee, with his own bank account as details for payment.

Another common method in the smaller business is for the payroll officer to create fake records and substitute their own bank account details for payment.

However, the most common method of creating a phantom employee is where a genuine employee leaves your employ but the line manager does not notify payroll of the termination. Instead of submitting a termination notice the manager puts through a change of details form and redirects the phantom employee's pay into their own account.

How do you prevent phantom employees? The first step is to identify managers who can employ staff and ensure that the payroll clerk is not one of them. Next, instigate an office process requiring that all new employees, with no exceptions, be interviewed by a human resource management or payroll staff member to ensure that the TFN declaration is correctly completed and that the employee's details are correctly entered into the system. Any changes to the employee's details, especially change of bank details, should be presented to the payroll officer by the employee themselves. Managers will attempt to get around this requirement, and if they do, they should be brought back into line in the sternest way.

In smaller firms, you should instigate a 'meet and greet' policy for all new employees. This handshake policy ensures all new employees actually exist. If a line manager tries to get around this policy they must be quickly brought back into line.

Records manipulation

This example shows how records manipulation can occur.

Example 4: payroll fraud

You employ a payroll clerk, Alice, for $25 per hour for a 35-hour week. She performs her job very well and you start to trust her to handle the payroll process. Alice cannot meet her mortgage payments, however, and is about to lose her house. All she needs is an extra $70 per week.

Alice's solution is to change her payroll records to pay herself $28 per hour. This results in an extra $105 per week, which after tax gives her more than the $70 she needs. Problem solved!

The big question is how would you pick up changes to the payroll records such as paying overtime that was never done or allowances that are not due? You must ensure that at each payday all of your payroll records are reviewed for changes in base rates and compared with source documents such as timesheets for any additional items. Often such verification procedures, or internal controls, can be built into normal business processes.

CHAPTER 12

Running a business through a family discretionary trust

Key area we will cover in this chapter

▶ Family discretionary trusts

Defined terms we will introduce

Trust: (an old English concept) created by a trust deed similar to a will

Trustee: the person who controls the distribution of the trust income (business taxable profits) and the trust corpus (capital, as in capital gain)

Beneficiary: any family member up to three generations either side of a nominated individual, usually the business owner

Discretionary: the ability to apply income to anyone nominated beneficiary (family member)

Personal excursion income (PSI): income from your own efforts, such as wages and wage substitutes, as distinct to passive income from investments, such as dividends and interest

This chapter provides only a very limited and general overview of the taxation concept of a family trust as it might be used to legitimately minimise your business's taxation liability. Our discussion will be limited to what are known as *family discretionary trusts*, as used to minimise business taxation, and within that limitation will only discuss the topic in very general terms. For a full and detailed discussion, see *Family Trusts*, 5th edition, which I had the pleasure of co-authoring with N.E. Renton.

First let me be very plain: trusts are a very old common law concept that has been manipulated beyond recognition in order to be used as a tax minimisation vehicle. They do not follow any rules of logic, only common law built up over centuries, modified for our purposes by the taxation administration acts. It should be noted at this point that the tax laws in regard to trusts for the most part do not tell you how to run a trust but rather what you cannot do. They are an anti-avoidance mechanism aimed at reining in the most flagrant abuses while allowing the general tax minimisation strategy to remain.

What is a family discretionary trust?

In the simplest terms a trust is similar to a partnership in which all members of your family can be considered as partners, but unlike in a partnership, trust partners (who are referred to as *beneficiaries*) have no say in running the business. Again, unlike a partnership, where the partners' share is fixed by the partnership agreement, in the case of a trust you can, at your discretion, funnel the taxable income from your business as you see fit in order to minimise your tax bill. The controlling mechanism of a trust, similar to a partnership agreement, is called the *trust deed*.

So how does it work? Let us assume that you are a small business owner running a very successful business as either a sole proprietor or a partnership with your spouse called Len's Web Services. As a sole proprietor, all of the taxation liability for your business income rests with you. If you are in partnership with your spouse then they can share some of the tax burden, but the Tax Office has very strict rules about sharing business income with non-participating spouses. This limits your opportunity to split your income.

You approach your tax accountant, who suggests setting up a family trust.

Firstly your accountant will set up a Pty Ltd company and either make you the sole director or make both you and your spouse directors. It is through this 'trustee' company that you will control the business. The name of the company can be anything you wish but it would usually be the business name, such as Len's Web Services Pty Ltd.

Next your accountant will create the trust. This is a simple matter of creating a trust deed that has all of the legal instructions needed to run the trust, and they will then give (or in trust terms *settle*) an amount of $10 onto this trust by banking it in a bank account in the name of the trust. The name of the trust can be anything you wish—for example, The McDonald Family Trust. The name of the bank account and the name on all of your business documents will be something like Len's Web Services Pty Ltd as Trustee for The McDonald Family Trust. It is through the company that you will undertake all of your business transactions, but with the company acting in its capacity as trustee, not in its own right. The company itself will be considered as a dormant trustee company only.

Then all of your business assets will be transferred (*gifted*, in trust terms) into the trust. You have to be careful at this stage as there can be capital gains tax issues with the disposal of business assets.

Finally you will make an irrevocable family trust election (or revocable only in very special circumstances) and you are then operational. A *family trust election* (FTE) must specify a *primary individual* (normally you as the business owner), whose family group (grandparents through to grandchildren) can receive distributions from the trust without penalty. Anyone outside the family or any family members who themselves use company or trust structures are 'normally' excluded (by a penalty tax regime) from the trust distribution. The FTE will also allow the trust to utilise trust losses without having to prove compliance with the trust loss measures, which are designed to prevent trust loss trading. It also simplifies dividend imputation streaming.

The end result is that:

▶ you are now at the centre of the business, running the show; you are called the trustee, or more correctly the *director of the trustee company*

▶ your business assets are now trust assets and are called to *objects of the trust*

▶ all of your family members for three generations either side of you are now your non-participating partners, called *beneficiaries*, who really have no control at all over your business or its income

▶ you can now allocate your business income to your family members as you see fit in order to minimise the overall tax bill of your business

▶ your only limitation is the provisions of the trust deed, which in many ways is similar to a partnership agreement.

Taxation income streaming

We must first set a number of ground rules in regard to our discussion of the taxation of trust income. A trust is not a separate taxable entity for income tax purposes. It is for GST and FBT, but we will discuss this later.

The number one golden rule is that trust income is calculated as if the trust were a resident taxpayer in respect of its taxable income and allowable deductions, as if it was a sole proprietor in business, but without any rebates and so on. The fact that the trustee is a company has no bearing on the calculation of the income of the trust. The company is simply there as a shield and has no role to play in the business itself.

The income of the trust (business) is taxed in the hands of the beneficiary (family member) to whom it has been allocated and it is taxed in the year the income was earned by the trust, not the year in which it is allocated to the individual. In tax terms, where the beneficiary is presently entitled to that income—that is, a trustee resolution has nominated a certain amount of the business income to that individual—that individual has the right to demand payment. It is this right of payment that can be a sticking point in some family situations.

The next rule is that whenever income is distributed to a beneficiary, subject to the provisions of the trust deed, the income retains its nature or character in the beneficiary's hands. For example, a capital gain made by the business can be allocated as a capital gain to a family member and subject to the 50 per cent discount rule, even though the trust is controlled by a company and companies cannot use the 50 per cent discount. Another example is in regard to any dividends that you the business may receive: the imputation credits will flow along with the dividend to the beneficiary, who can use those imputation credits to offset their 'other income' tax bill.

It is because of the income streaming benefits of the trust that an annual allocation of the business income has to be made, in the form of a trustee resolution to the nominated beneficiaries that will split up the various components—Joe gets the capital gain and Mary the dividends, with Harry getting straight business income, for example.

By dividing the business income among family members, not only by dollar value but also by type, it is possible to make substantial savings in the overall income tax bill of the business. However, if any amount is not allocated—that is, there is some income left over—then the trustee will be taxed on this income at a penalty rate equal to the top individual marginal rate, irrespective of the fact that the trustee may be a company. Similarly, if any amount over the base (which is explained later) is allocated to a minor, then that excess is also taxed in the hands of the trustee at the penalty rate.

Problems you can encounter

The first major problem is one created by the Tax Administration Act, and that is a provision that requires that 100 per cent of the trust income be distributed to the beneficiaries or a penalty rate of tax will be applied to any shortfall. That penalty rate is set at the top marginal rate for an individual, currently 49 per cent. This is paid by the trustee in their capacity as trustee, therefore corporate trustees are still required to pay this individual penalty rate rather than the lower company rate, currently 28.5 per cent.

There are two problems with the construction of this section of the Tax Act: first is the problem of taxable income versus business income; secondly, the definition of income in the Tax Act contains both income and capital components, *income* and *corpus* in trust terms. This section can also cause problems where there is a subsequent revision to the accounts, say through an unexpected refund or as a result of a tax audit that results in an increase in the business income to which no beneficiary is 'presently entitled'—that is, income that has not been specifically allocated to a family member.

The resolution of all of these problems lies in the trust deed, but first a little trust history to set the scene.

Trusts were originally a vehicle of the British nobility to avoid death duties. In the trust deed it was normal to allocate the physical estate to the eldest son, but to allocate income from the estate to the siblings, as a living to the younger sons and as a form of ongoing dowry to the daughters. Hence the distinction in trust law between the capital (corpus) of the trust and the income derived from that capital.

It was therefore common for trust deeds to allocate the income of the trust specifically to one class of beneficiaries and the corpus of the trust to another. This causes immense difficulties with income streaming—that is, your ability to allocate different types of 'taxable' income to nominated beneficiaries—and should be avoided at all costs.

When capital gains tax was introduced in Australia in 1985 any capital gain was to be included in a person's normal taxable income and taxed accordingly. Hence taxable income can have components of both capital and income (in the normal sense).

The way in which to overcome these problems is first to define income in the trust deed as income in accordance with the provisions of the income tax assessment acts as they may be modified from time to time. This simple mechanism will overcome the problems of accounting profit versus taxable income and will allow the streaming of all trust income to the beneficiaries irrespective of its makeup.

The next mechanism to include is a default beneficiary, one who is allocated not an amount or percentage of the trust income but rather any income left over after the allocations have been made. This default beneficiary will then be 'presently entitled' to any trust income that may be generated after the trustee resolution by some unexpected event and will overcome the penalty tax that could apply to such income.

Personal excursion income (PSI)

A family trust can only distribute income from trading activities to its beneficiaries. If you make money from your own personal excursion, then you will be taxed on this income irrespective of the business structure. It is a form of flow-through taxation.

If you are unsure whether or not your business is one that generates PSI income, then you need to discuss the various options with your accountant.

Children as beneficiaries

Basically a child under 18 who is not in full-time employment is not a good candidate for a trust income distribution. Penalty rates of tax pertain to the income applied to any child receiving more than a set amount, currently $416, other than that from their own personal excursion. This was not always the case. For example, in the 2011 tax year you could utilise a low-income rebate that raised this amount to $3333; however, that concession was withdrawn in regard to unearned income from the 2012 tax year and onwards. I should stress at this point that this discussion is in regard to the distribution of business income to family members. Separate rules apply to trust distribution to children with disabilities.

The best advice I can give is to leave minors out of any calculation you may do in regard to the benefits of entering a family trust arrangement.

Social security and other family benefit payments

When you allocate an amount of income to a family member, that income becomes income to that member for all purposes, whether or not it was actually paid to the family member. Most social security payments are means tested, which could result in a reduction in payments made to that member. It could also affect payments such as Youth Allowance, New Start and Ausstudy.

Before allocating an amount to a family member you must ensure that you (and your accountant) are fully aware of that family member's financial situation. Failure to take this into account could have serious consequences.

The costs associated with trust accounting

You may have noticed along the way the major downside to family trusts—that is, the accountancy fees incurred, first in setting up the trust and then the ongoing fees associated with all of the documentation required, including the number of annual tax returns, not only for your business but also for each member of your family who has received a trust distribution. If you are not very careful, the tax you save could be more than offset by the increase in accountancy fees incurred in running the trust.

Other taxes

When you are in business, whether through a trust or any other structure, you still have to register for an ABN and lodge a quarterly BAS in which you account for the GST and withholding taxes. You will also have to account for any FBT liability with an annual FBT return if required.

When we talk of family trusts and tax minimisation we are really only talking about income taxes, including capital gains tax, and not about all of the other taxes and charges you face as a business proprietor. All of the other impositions will be handled in exactly the same way as they would have been had you stayed in business as a sole proprietor.

Are trusts worth the effort?

Restructuring your business into a trust will have no effect on the day-to-day running of your business. It will increase the work required by your tax accountant at year's end and will require the accountant to be fully conversant with all of the financial affairs of every member of the family in order to advise you on the most tax-effective distribution of the business income. Some family members might find those conditions overly intrusive.

Trusts are also very time consuming and therefore expensive to run in terms of the accountant's fees. Does your business generate an income, now and into the future, to the extent that these extra costs will be more than offset by the benefits gained?

Could these benefits be as easily achieved with a company structure using a combination of salary to the directors and dividend with imputation credits to the shareholders?

Appendix A: Effective life schedule

When a small business purchases an asset it is recorded in their accounting records and depreciated at a set rate. If.the business is a micro business then that rate is 15 per cent for the first year and 30 per cent based on the diminishing value for subsequent years. If the small business has an income in excess of $2 million per year then it must depreciate the asset based on the asset's *effective life*, usually using the diminishing value method.

The effective life of an asset can be determined by the business itself or you can use the 'safe harbour' provisions of effective life as published by the Tax Office at the time you purchased the asset. If you determine the effective life yourself you can be called upon to justify your position, whereas the Tax Office will accept an allowable deduction based on its own effective life schedule.

Table AA1 (overleaf) lists examples taken in the order they appear from *Taxation Ruling 2013/14*. This ruling is updated annually and you should refer to the most current ruling when setting the life of any asset.

Table AA1: Effective life examples (excerpted from *Taxation Ruling 2013/14*)

Asset description	Effective life	Equivalent %
All-terrain vehicles used in farming	5	40
Motorcycle used in farming	5	40
Digital printers (ink, thermal or toner based)	5	40
Concrete mixers and walk-behind trowels	5	40
Mobile light and medium cranes	15	13.3
Dozers and front-end loaders	9	22.2
Forklifts	11	18.2
Power hand tools—air (includes nail guns)	5	40
Power hand tools—electric	5	40
Power hand tools—battery	3	66.7
Hand tools generally	10	20
Carpets in office	8	25
Caravans	$6^2/_3$	30
Computers	4	50
Laptops	3	66.7
Bookcases and office cabinets—timber	15	13.3
Bookcases and office cabinets—metal	20	10
Chairs	10	20
Desks	20	10
Reception furniture	10	20
Tables—boardroom	20	10
Tables—general	10	20
Workstation desks and partitions	20	10

Asset description	Effective life	Equivalent %
Motor vehicles—buses over 3.5 tonnes	15	13.3
—cars	8	25
—hire or traveller's	5	40
—taxi	4	50
—minibuses	12	16.7
—light commercial	12	16.7
—trucks over 3.5 tonnes	15	13.3
—trailers under 4.5 tonnes	10	20
—trailers over 4.5 tonnes	15	13.3
Cash register	10	20
Weighing machines and labelling	10	20

The effective life examples above are converted into a percentage by dividing it into 200, as explained in chapter 4, on capital allowances. A 12-year life would equate to 16.7 per cent depreciation rate; a 5-year life to 40 per cent; and so on.

Appendix B: Tax rates, 2014–15

The following rates for 2014–15 apply from 1 July 2014.

Australia's tax year runs from 1 July to 30 June, and therefore the 2014–2015 tax year was from 1 July 2014 to 30 June 2015 and is often referred to simply as the 2015 tax year.

Company tax rate

The company tax rate from 1 July 2014 is 28.5 per cent, reduced from 30 per cent. For large companies this will offset the cost of the government's 1.5 per cent paid parental leave levy.

Fringe Benefits Tax

The FBT rate is linked to the top marginal rate and will be set at 47 per cent for the 2014–2015 FBT year (1 April 2014 to 31 March 2015) and will rise to 49 per cent for the 2015–2016 FBT year (1 April 2015 to 31 March 2016).

Resident individuals

Table AB1 applies to your total income from all sources, whether in Australia or overseas.

Table AB1: income tax rates for resident individuals

Taxable income	Tax on this income
0 – $18 200	Nil
$18 201 – $37 000	19c for each $1 over $18 200
$37 001 – $80 000	$3572 plus 32.5c for each $1 over $37 000
$80 001 – $180 000	$17 547 plus 37c for each $1 over $80 000
$180 001 and over	$54 547 plus 47c for each $1 over $180 000

The above rates *do not* include the Medicare levy.

Medicare levy

The Medicare levy increased from 1.5 per cent to 2 per cent from the 1 July 2014. A Medicare care levy of 2 per cent of your taxable income applied to most individuals earning over $20 542 and for families from $34 367 plus $3156 for each dependent child.

The top marginal tax rate

The top marginal rate for an individual is therefore 47 per cent plus 2 per cent Medicare—that is, 49 per cent from the 1 July 2014. Prior to this it was 46.5 per cent.

Tax rate for children's 'unearned' income (for example, trust distributions)

Minors under 18 have a somewhat complex tax structure. Income from their own personal excursion, welfare payments (Centrelink) and the like are taxed at 'normal' rates and low income rebates apply. Unearned income is taxed as in table AB2, and no low income rebate can apply to these distributions.

Table AB2: tax rates on unearned income

Unearned income	Tax on this income
$0 – $416	Nil
$417 – $1307	Nil + 66 per cent of the excess over $416
Over $1307	45 per cent of the total amount of income that is not excepted income

The latest tax rates can be downloaded from the Tax Office website at www.ato.gov.au or from my website at www.tpabusiness.com.au.

Index

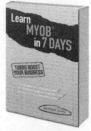